Tacky's Tugs

TREVOL c1926 towing a 'wooden wall' (ex-RN training or accommodation hulk) at Millbay. The steam towing winch can be seen with the mate standing at the winch controls aft of the funnel.
W. J. REYNOLDS

Tacky's Tugs

W. J. Reynolds Ltd of Torpoint

by

Captain Stephen Carter

TWELVEHEADS PRESS

TRURO 2008

The majority of the fleet off Torpoint c1966, left to right TREVOL (2) *and* ALEXANDRA, CARBEILE, TACTFUL (2) *and* WOLSDON. *This picture allows a good comparison to be made of two Cox built tugs, the* ALEXANDRA *built 1902 and the* TREVOL *built 1921. The* ALEXANDRA *has probably just towed the* TREVOL *from the slipway at Carbeile Creek.* PAUL RICHARDS

TWELVEHEADS PRESS

First published 2008 by Twelveheads Press
ISBN 978 0 906294 66 6
British Library Cataloguing-in-Publication Data.
A catalogue record for this book is available from the British Library.
Printed by The Amadeus Press, Cleckheaton, West Yorkshire.

CONTENTS

Preface 7

Chapter one An enterprise is born 11

Chapter two Years of expansion 19

Chapter three Growth and consolidation 23

Chapter four Opportunity and expansion 31

Chapter five The old order changeth 47

Chapter six Second World War 53

Chapter seven The post war period 59

Chapter eight Changing fortunes 71

Chapter nine Eddystone Rocks and concrete blocks 81

Chapter ten Big ships and Bovril Boats 89

Chapter eleven The final years 107

Chapter twelve The family 119

Chapter thirteen Horses 123

Postscipt 125

Appendix one Crew list of the *Antony* 1940 132

Appendix two Apprentice indenture 134

Appendix three The match of the season 137

Acknowledgements 139

Index 141

The City of Plymouth is probably one of the best known of all British ports, and over the centuries has played its part in many wars, campaigns and battles. Sir Francis Drake sailed from Plymouth, to repulse the Spanish Armada, and Plymouth was the departure port of the Pilgrim Fathers. Plymouth has been the home port for many thousands of ships, both naval and merchant, and as a port had, and still has, many advantages, the most important being its sheltered location and comparatively easy access from sea and land.

The history of Plymouth and its dockyards, naval and merchant has been very well documented over the years, and there is a wealth of information available to those who seek further knowledge. I do not propose, or indeed could not hope to even outline all the historical events which made Plymouth a great port, but only to try and trace the story of a small but important cog in that overall history.

Apart from the great Naval Dockyards that spread along the Devon banks of the River Tamar, there were a number of major commercial docks, the London and South Western Railway developed commercial wharfs at Stonehouse, the Great Western Railway developed Millbay Docks, Sutton Harbour was owned by a private company, as were the later Victoria Wharfs, and Cattedown Wharfs on the Cattewater were also developed by private enterprise. Along with these docks there were a host of smaller wharfs and quays both around the Cattewater and Hamoaze, and occurring right up to the tidal limits of the rivers Tamar, Tavy and Lynher.

Whilst at school on my native Isle of Man, I was, in the mid 1960s, a member of the Naval Section of the Combined Cadet Force. One summer I took the opportunity to attend a coxswain's course at the naval training establishment *HMS Raleigh* at Torpoint. I journeyed on a travel warrant by boat and train to Plymouth's North Road station where I, and some cadets from other units, were collected by coach, which then proceeded to Torpoint by way of the chain ferry. I was 16 years old and had owned my own boats since the age of 11 and lived for boats. Crossing the Tamar on the ferry, I observed a fleet of somewhat antiquated looking steam tugs lying on a trot of moorings near the ferry (the only other tugs I had seen at this time being in Liverpool, which although some were still steam powered, appeared much more modern). And the sight of these aged tugs was a memory filed in my mind for many years.

This book attempts to tell the story of these tugs, which were part of an enterprise, a family business lasting for nearly a hundred years, and which in its day was as much a part of Plymouth's maritime scene as Plymouth Hoe. Rather interestingly though, this enterprise was not based at Plymouth, but at the Cornish town of Torpoint, linked to Plymouth then as now by the aforementioned chain ferries across the River Tamar.

W. J. Reynolds came to Torpoint from Torquay and he, his sons and grandsons built up a business which in its day became the biggest civilian employer in Torpoint. They had a fleet of tugs and barges engaged on a wide variety of work, had a marine engineering business and slipway, a farm selling produce locally, a coal yard and builders merchants, and for a time in the early years a small fleet of passenger boats. They came to own the last fleet of coal fired steam tugs operating in Britain, and were also the last people in Devon and Cornwall to use heavy horses on commercial haulage. During nearly a century of operations they never bought a new tug or barge, but were adept at keeping elderly vessels and plant in good working order. In common with many family businesses, they looked after their employees, many giving a working lifetime to the firm, and those now retired employees still with us look back on times working for W. J. Reynolds with pride and affection. The company was invariably known to everybody in the Plymouth area as 'Tacky Reynolds' for reasons now obscure.

Today there is virtually nothing left and a visitor to Torpoint would have difficulty in finding any traces of this once prosperous enterprise. Luckily, at the time of writing, there are still a number of retired employees living in the area, as well as several family members; and meeting and talking to these people, all of whom were most generous with their time and reminiscences, has helped greatly to build up a better picture of the firm of W. J. Reynolds Ltd. However, whilst personal reminiscences add greatly to the substance of the book, charting the early years has been a little more difficult to achieve. Few company or family records remain and the heavy bombing of Plymouth during the Blitz of the Second World War destroyed many sources of information, notably newspaper cuttings and photographic archives. As a result, it may well be that some of the dates in the early chronology of the enterprise may not be entirely accurate. When the firm closed, the directors spent several days emptying the papers in the office and burning them in a big bonfire at Carbeile Mill; consequently there are very few original records from the company left in existence. No book on a subject such as this can cover every detail, and any mistakes which may have inadvertently appeared, are entirely mine.

NOTES

In the text various abbreviations are used which require explanation. Where the dimensions of vessels are given they are in feet and tenths of feet as the vessel is described in the official registration papers. So to take for example the tug *Carbeile*, her dimensions are listed as follows, 77.6 x 21.6 x 10.6 feet, this gives the length as 77 feet and 6 tenths of a foot, beam 21 feet and 6 tenths of a foot and depth of hull (not draft) at 10 feet and 6 tenths of a foot. However, the actual length of the *Carbeile* was about 83 feet, the reason for this is that under a peculiarity of the registration system, the length is measured from the after side of the stem post to the forward side of the stern post, and in the case of a tug with a counter stern, the stern would overhang the sternpost by several feet. The tonnage of a particular vessel is given as the gross registered tonnage. This has nothing to do with the actual weight of the vessel. 1 gross ton is equal to 100 cubic feet of internal space. So to take the *Carbeile* again, her gross tonnage was 110 but her actual weight or displacement tonnage was 196 tons (i.e. if you wanted to lift the *Carbeile* out of the water with a crane, then the crane would have to be able to lift 196 tons).

Let us now turn to horse power. In the early days a uniform system of measuring the power of a steam engine was derived and was obtained by measuring the swept volume of the cylinders. This gave a term known as Nominal Horse Power, NHP in the book. However, NHP did not take into account the steam pressure and so that as boilers improved and steam pressures became higher, two engines with the same nominal horse power but with different boiler pressures, would produce different powers, so a new system was developed which measured engine power using a device called an indicator. This gave a series of readings which could then be translated into the true power of the engine, or Indicated Horse Power, IHP in the book. Once again to take the *Carbeile*, her NHP was 44 but her IHP was 550. When the internal combustion engine came onto the scene, they were usually measured in Brake Horse Power, the rating being achieved by attaching the engine to a 'brake' or dynamometer which loaded the engine and measured the power. The only vessel in Reynolds' ownership that this system was used on was the launch *Vussel*. Boiler steam pressures are recorded in 'pounds per square inch' or PSI.

As the book charts the history of a firm operating mainly in the Plymouth area, I have used three shortened names as used locally. When the term Dockyard is used, it refers to the Royal Naval Dockyards at Devonport and when the term the Sound is used, it refers to Plymouth Sound. Finally when the term the Breakwater is used, it refers to Plymouth Breakwater, in Plymouth Sound.

Apart from the last year, W. J. Reynolds operated in a time of pre-decimal coinage in Britain. Therefore throughout the narrative monetary sums are recorded in pounds shillings and pence. For younger readers not familiar with the old coinage, £1 comprised of 20 shillings and each shilling comprised of 12 old pennies £.s.d.; so each pound had 240 old pence.

In the early years prior to becoming a limited company, the tugs and barges were owned by individual members of the family and others, but as they were all operated effectively as part of one fleet I have treated them as such in the text.

Stephen Carter

SIMPSON, STRICKLAND & CO., Ltd., DARTMOUTH.

TYPE No. II.

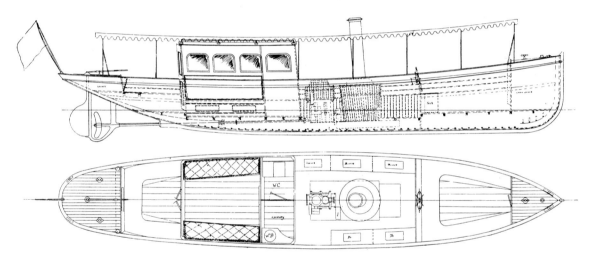

Dimensions   ...   43' × 8' × 4' 2"

Simpson Strickland & Co Ltd of Dartmouth were the builders of both the LINK and DAINTY, two of Reynold's earliest vessels. This general arrangement diagram of one of their a standard steam launches resembles the LINK. Simpson Strickland launches were usually fitted with a Kingdom boiler, a special vertical launch boiler designed for small steam launches. ALAN KITTRIDGE COLLECTION

CHAPTER ONE

AN ENTERPRISE IS BORN

William John Reynolds was born in Torquay, Devon, in 1854. Family tradition records that at least one of his grandfathers, John Reynolds, had been a mariner, not an unusual calling in this part of the world, and his father William was recorded as being a butcher on a warship, who came ashore to become a slaughterman. William senior moved with his family to live at Arthur Terrace, Torpoint in about 1863. However, in his early career, W. J. Reynolds does not seem to have followed in any of his forebears maritime footsteps.

In the census of 1881 William John Reynolds is recorded as living at 18 Fore Street, Antony (this requires some explanation, Antony being the parish in which Torpoint is situated). The address should correctly have been 18 Fore Street, Torpoint, in the Parish of Antony. He is described as a draper aged 26 and living with him were his wife Rebecca M. Reynolds aged 25, born in Devonport and their first child Wilfred J. Reynolds aged one and born in Torpoint. William's wife Rebecca was the daughter of a noted barge owning family, the Martins of St Dominic. Jumping ahead 10 years, in the 1891 census W. J. Reynolds was living at Carbeile Mill, Torpoint, with his wife Rebecca and four sons, and was described as a farmer and contractor. In another ten years, in 1901, W. J. was described as a Government Contractor and three of his four sons appeared to each have been apprenticed in Devonport Dockyard, to a trade allied with nautical matters: 21 year old Wilfred J. was a coppersmith; 18 year old Claude W. G. was a shipwright; and 17 year old Arthur Basil, a ship fitter (iron). In addition there was 15 year old Walter Fearnley and daughter Cora Ernestine born in 1891. Rebecca is now shown as being born in Stoke, Devonport. One of the difficulties in tracing the early years is the lack of recorded information and much of the following comes from family recollections.

It is not known exactly when William decided that drapery was not for him, but sometime in the early 1880s he seems to have become a farmer and carter, owning horses and carts used for the carriage of diverse materials around the neighbourhood. Carbeile Mill was a tide mill situated at the head of Carbeile Creek on St Johns Lake on the outskirts of Torpoint and it came with about 26 acres of fertile agricultural land and a small tidal quay. It had been built in 1819 and had an extensive mill pond; which had been created by damming off the upper part of the tidal creek. At the head of the creek was a small stone quay which served a stone quarry and to maintain access the dam when built had to incorporate a lock gate, to allow barges to reach the quay at high water. Tide mills, which by their nature were always situated on the shoreline of a tidal river, worked by the high tide filling up a pond at which time a sluice gate was closed impounding the water. As the tide ebbed the water from the pond was released and drove the water wheel which in turn powered the milling machinery. At Carbeile the main sluices were situated under the floor of the mill buildings. By the 1880s small tide mills were often going out of use for their intended purpose, larger modern steam powered roller mills at large ports were more efficient, and it might have been that the mill at Carbeile was available at an attractive price because of this. There is no record of William operating the mill as a mill, later, as will be recorded, the mill pond was filled in and the buildings became the engineering base for the family business The land, however, was farmed and the Mill Farm remained an integral part of the business until the end.

William Reynolds was obviously a man of some enterprise as he began a business selling fresh farm produce to the various naval training and active ships moored in the Hamoaze (the area of water lying between Devon and Cornwall at the seaward end of the River Tamar). This business prospered to such an extent that Mill Farm could not keep up with demand and produce was purchased from other farmers to fulfil the need. It seems that this trade led to Reynolds' first vessel, a small steam launch named the *Bessie*, which was used to carry the fresh produce out to the various ships. Unfortunately, extensive research has failed to find any details of the *Bessie* which was probably unregistered.

Family tradition recalls that in 1882 William embarked on a venture which was to secure the long term financial future of the family business. Devonport Dockyard was expanding and many sailors were based there. Apart from the naval ratings and officers there was also a rapidly expanding civilian workforce employed in the Dockyard. At this time the dockyard machinery, heating in the various buildings and houses, and more importantly the naval ships, were all coal fired, so there was a vast quantity of ash to be disposed of, as well as ordinary refuse. The contract to dispose of this waste had been held by a Plymouth concern, Little & Co, but the contract was now secured by W. J. Reynolds. Some of the ashes may have been disposed of by loading into horses and carts, supplied by Reynolds, and tipped at handy landfill sites inside or adjacent to the Dockyard, some may have been tipped into sailing barges for disposal at sea, once again it is not entirely clear. However, as far as can be traced, apart from the little launch *Bessie*, there are no records of Reynolds owning any substantial boats or barges until 1894, and these purchases were small passenger steamers. However, in his obituary many years later, it is recorded that he embarked on the disposal of refuse from naval ships and Dockyard joining his father, using rowing boats and sailing barges. The way that the obituary is written might suggest that it was William senior, who negotiated the first contracts, but it is more likely that the journalist writing the obituary was confused and it was William junior. To date, no records of any of these small vessels have come to light. It is also possible

that having secured the Dockyard contract, Reynolds supplied the horses and carts and sub contracted the sea dumping to someone else. What did start at this time, and became quite famous in Plymouth and Torpoint, was the sight every morning of the Shire and Clydesdale heavy horses in full harness, each led by a horseman, walking from the Mill Farm at Torpoint where they were stabled, onto the chain ferry and crossing to the Dockyard to collect their carts and spend the day carting refuse within the Dockyard before returning to the farm *via* the ferry in the evening. The carts were left unhitched in the Dockyard unless they required some repair or maintenance when they would be brought back to the mill. As an aside, in some official documents of the time including the registration papers for various vessels, Carbeile was spelt Carbeal.

In 1894 the chain ferries between Devonport and Torpoint finished at 9pm every evening and travellers wishing to cross after this time had to make use of rowing or sailing boats owned by local watermen. This service apparently proved less than satisfactory and W. J. Reynolds decided that this gave him another business opportunity. He purchased two small wooden screw passenger steamers, the *Link* and *Dainty*, and these were put to work running a foot passenger ferry service between Torpoint and Devonport. During the summer months they were also employed in running excursions. Whether these two boats were used for towing remains unclear but surviving photographs suggest that they were not very suitable for towage work. In order to raise money, possibly to pay for the *Link* and *Dainty*, or to raise capital for some other purpose, the *Dainty* was mortgaged in 1896, but the business was kept within the family, the mortgagees being Thomas Edwin Reynolds, George Henry Reynolds, Albert Edward Reynolds, and Walter Samuel Reynolds, all of Torpoint, and younger brothers of William John Reynolds. The passenger trade

Torpoint passenger steamer LINK with DAINTY just visible alongside slipway. It is clear from the photographs that these were typical small passenger launches and unsuitable for towing operations.
ALAN KITTRIDGE
COLLECTION

Paddle steamer
MARGUERITE heads
up the River Tamar
to Weir Head.
ALAN KITTRIDGE
COLLECTION

must have looked promising as in 1898 a larger passenger vessel was purchased. This was the only paddle steamer owned by Reynolds, the iron built *Marguerite*, which had been launched in Cubitt Town, London in 1879 for the London Asylums Board, but at the time of Reynolds' purchase was owned by Walter Hearse of Oxford. Reynolds put this vessel into the excursion trade on the River Tamar, operating with his other passenger boats under the banner of the Torpoint Steamboat Company. At this time there was plenty of competition in the excursion business from both John Parson's Millbrook Steamboat Company and the bigger Saltash Three Towns & District Steamboat Company, the latter operating powerful tugs as well as a fleet of passenger steamers. Reynolds' involvement in the passenger trade was brought to an untimely end. In 1901, the Torpoint Ferry Company, who owned the landing rights at Torpoint, substantially increased the landing dues payable by Reynolds and this reduced the viability of his operations. This appeared to be a poorly concealed manoeuvre to get rid of Reynolds as the ferry company shortly afterwards purchased two passenger ferries, one second hand, the *Volta* which commenced operations in 1902, and one new, the *Lady Beatrice*, launched in 1904, and put them to work on the pedestrian ferry service. They had apparently realised that Reynolds was doing quite well out of the ferrying and presumably wanted to take over this profitable trade.

Whether as a result of losing the ferry business, or competition in the excursion business, or possibly a combination of both, Reynolds gave up the passenger trade and none of the boats operated as passenger steamers after 1901. At this time the Millbrook Steamboat company and the Saltash company were engaged in a cut throat price war, each trying to run the other out of the excursion business. The fate of the *Marguerite* has not been traced but the *Dainty* and *Link* appear to have been used in some capacity until eventually laid up to rot at Carbeile Creek, the *Dainty*'s registration being closed on the 10 May 1904.

The next vessels acquired by Reynolds were capable of towing. The *Lorna* was a 44 feet long iron vessel built in Plymouth in 1877, fully decked and powered by a steam engine of 12 NHP driving a single propeller. The only known photograph of the *Lorna* shows her with temporary wire rope guard rails on top of the low bulwarks suggesting a passenger carrying role. It is not thought that the vessel was in Reynolds' ownership when the photograph was taken and it would have been an easy matter to modify the *Lorna* for towing work. Once again, researches have failed to show exactly when Reynolds purchased this vessel. The other vessel was slightly smaller. The 40 feet long wooden *Mascotte* was built in Plymouth and was powered by a 6 NHP engine developing 25 IHP, and was purchased in 1903. As Reynolds had given up his passenger business by this date, it seems a reasonable assumption that these vessels were probably used for towing, and as long as they were running with the tide, would have been powerful enough to tow small barges. The *Mascotte* was purchased in 1903 by W. J. Reynolds, mortgaged to one Henry Tucker of

The LORNA, *a much more substantial vessel, alongside another Plymouth tug, the* REINDEER, *in Sutton Harbour. The* REINDEER *was lost coming down the River Tamar from Calstock when she ran onto the steep bank on a sharp bend near Cargreen on a falling tide and eventually rolled over as the tide receded.*
MIKE DOHERTY

Athenaeum Place, Plymouth. In 1912 the ownership was transferred from Tucker (Did he call in the mortgage?) to Wilfred Reynolds and one Samuel Hugh Duff, and immediately re mortgaged to the West of England Loan and Discharge Co. Who Samuel Duff was has not been ascertained but he was joint owner in a number of Reynolds' vessels up to and during the Great War period.

One trade that Reynolds was well placed to enter was the towing of sailing ships up the River Tamar to the various quays such as Calstock, Gawton, New Quay, Morwhellham and others. For many years the Saltash Three Towns & District Steamboat company had stationed a purpose built steam tug, the *Victoria*, at Calstock, but this had been sold and the remains of the trade may well have been taken by Reynolds.

Although business from the river quays was in terminal decline, there was still some business to be obtained and another trade which lasted for much longer, until well after the Second World War, was in road stone from various quarries on the River Lynher and its tributary River Tiddy to quays in the Plymouth area. One quarry later owned a fleet of 200 ton capacity dumb barges, named somewhat incongruously after precious stones, which were used for carrying stone, often to Pomphlett, or to ships too large to navigate up the river, and there is a picture in existence (regrettably too small for reproduction) in which *Wolsdon* is towing a dumb barge up the Cattewater towards Pomphlett.

The Dockyard contract involved removing large quantities of ashes, which in the early days were loaded into barges in Moon Cove, just to the north of the Torpoint Ferry's Devonport landing, and at some stage Reynolds reached an agreement to use these ashes to fill in the mill pond at Carbeile Mill. The only realistic way to transport these ashes would have been to load them into barges at the Dockyard, tow the barges to Carbeile Creek, and bring the barges through the lock gate into the mill pond at high water. The ashes could then be discharged. Exactly when this took place has not been ascertained, but one suggestion, which would seem extremely likely, is that the infilling took place during the Great War. It became too dangerous for the tugs and barges to proceed slowly out to sea, where they would have been easy targets for submarines or surface raiders. During the Great War the *Link* and *Lorna*, and possibly the *Dainty* as well, were moved through the lock gate into the mill pond and partially dismantled, the remains being buried under the ashes. The original plan had been to use the reclaimed land as a grazing field for the horses, but all four Reynolds brothers were keen sportsmen and supported and played football for Torpoint, and the field was eventually made into the sports and football ground it is today.

Prior to 1911 Reynolds owned several barges including a hopper barge named *Thames* and in 1909, again together with Samuel Hugh Duff, purchased two Portsmouth built hopper barges the *Jumbo* and the *Tap*. Both barges were mortgaged, the *Jumbo* to Henry Tucker of Athenaeum Place, Plymouth, and the *Tap* to the Naval Bank. Reynolds also appears to have had a good working relationship with a Plymouth stevedore and coal porter, John Haskell of White Lane, Plymouth, and his son Joseph.

The Haskells also owned barges, mostly old sailing ships stripped of their rigging such as the *Harry Herbert* and *Excelsior* (although these two vessels were not purchased by Haskell until the Second World War) and it is more than probable that Reynolds chartered some of them on occasions. Haskell's barges were much used for bunkering ships (with coal) and Reynold's tugs were employed to tow these barges to and from the ships to be bunkered.

As the Edwardian era drew to a close, W. J. Reynolds had become a man of some substance. He owned various vessels, Carbeile Mill, which was now used as an engineering base, the Mill Farm supplying fresh produce to the Navy, and held the lucrative contract for the disposal of ashes and waste from Devonport Dockyard. During this period two of his sons joined him in the business and it was no doubt this factor which prompted the purchase of more powerful tugs just prior to the Great War.

TOWAGE DISTANCES.

			Miles
From	Plymouth to	Salcombe	18
,,	,,	Fowey ..	21
,,	,,	Dartmouth	32
,,	,,	Falmouth	38
,,	,,	Brixham	38
,,	,,	Torquay ..	40
,,	,,	Teignmouth	45
,,	,,	Exmouth	50
,,	Dartmouth to Fowey ..		50
,,	Exmouth to Fowey ..		62
,,	Torquay to Fowey ..		56
,,	Teignmouth to Fowey ..		60
,,	Salcombe to Fowey ..		36
,,	Weymouth to Fowey ..		100
,,	Portland to Fowey ..		100

Printed and Published by
Parade Printing Works, Ltd. 20/21 Southside St
Plymouth
Telephone 64882

Page from a W. J. Reynolds tide table booklet for 1971.
DAVID MARTIN

The iron tug SAXON, *built at Falmouth in 1883. W. J. Reynolds' first purpose built tug.* W. J. REYNOLDS

CHAPTER TWO

YEARS OF EXPANSION

The next vessel purchased by Reynolds was a purpose built iron tug. The *Saxon* was 58 feet long and had been built in Falmouth in 1883 by Cox and Co. She was fitted with a compound steam engine of 14 NHP developing 90 IHP. She came to Torpoint on 1 July 1911 at a cost of £650, having been purchased from Falmouth tug owner William Rowe. The *Saxon* was registered in the name of Wilfred J. Reynolds, William's eldest son, confirming that he had joined his father in the business. The *Saxon* was a great advance on the earlier vessels, and in her days at Falmouth had been involved in many minor salvage jobs, which included assisting in the refloating of the Scilly Isles passenger steamer *Lady of the Isles*, which had run aground on rocks at Lamorna Cove in 1904.

That the dumping of the Dockyard waste at sea was taking place by this time is confirmed by summonsing of William Reynolds to appear before the Plymouth Police Courts on 14 February 1912 when he was charged with not going out to sea far enough to the designated dumping grounds to tip. An area outside Plymouth Sound had been designated as an area for dumping refuse at sea. As well as the Dockyard refuse, Plymouth Council also disposed of refuse by sea dumping; going far enough out to sea was supposed to stop the refuse being washed back inshore and onto the beaches and coasts. However, in bad weather with inshore winds, the temptation must have been to release the load closer to the land, which was apparently the case as Reynolds was convicted and fined £7.7s.3d.

At this point it might be time to describe in some detail the practical operation of the Devonport Dockyard refuse contract. As mentioned earlier the cart horses were stabled at Mill Farm and every morning up to 16 horses would cross on the chain ferry to the Dockyard. Once there each would be harnessed to a tipping cart and the horses and carts would make rounds of the extensive dockyards collecting the ashes and refuse in exactly the same fashion as bin men do today. The refuse would be hauled in the early days to two locations within the Dockyard where a hopper barge would be moored alongside a Dockyard wall under a shute. One shute was situated on the river wall of No 3 Basin between the basin entrance and the boat basin, the other was at the north end of the Dockyard in Weston Mill Lake on the river wall east of the coaling wharf on the north side of the No 6 or Prince of Wales Basin. In both locations the barges would remain afloat at all states of the tide. In later years only the shute by the No 3 basin was in use. The cart would then tip the refuse into the hopper barge. It was not an unusual occurrence for the horse to back up too much, or the cart tip too quickly and overbalance, which dragged both horse and cart into the hopper, sometimes with fatal consequences for the horse. When the barge was full, a tug collected the full barge, placed it in another temporary berth, and substituted an empty barge under the shute. The full barge would then be towed out into Plymouth Sound to the dumping ground in Whitsand Bay.

The hopper barge requires some explanation. A hopper barge was a type of vessel developed originally for disposing of mud dredged from harbours. Unlike a normal vessel, a hopper barge has opening doors in the bottom to drop the contents into the sea. Hopper barges normally have large airtight forepeak and afterpeak compartments. Down each side, built into the hull, are watertight tanks the full depth of the hull. These compartments and tanks give the required buoyancy. This leaves a rectangular space or hopper area in the middle of the barge in which the water level is the same as outside the barge. The cargo in the hopper area in the middle of the barge is retained by a series of hinged doors at the bottom of the hull and these are kept closed (but not watertight) by a series of heavy chains usually attached to a winding shaft or shafts. When the doors are closed, the refuse from the Dockyard could be tipped in and would remain in the barge displacing the water in the barge hold. When towed to sea the barge would have a crew of four men and when the dumping ground was reached the chains would be released, the bottom doors would open downwards and the load would drop out onto the sea bed. Because some of the refuse would be partially buoyant, it would not always drop out and each barge was equipped with a number of 20 feet long wooden poles and these were used to push the floating refuse down and through the doors. Whilst the dumping was taking place the tug would be towing the barge in a big circle to help wash the refuse out. If the weather was rough the refuse usually emptied quicker as the barge rolling about would help the refuse to drop out. In calm weather it could sometimes take several hours to empty the barge. Once empty the tug would start to tow the barge back and the crew on the barge would have to man the handles on the winding gear and laboriously wind up the chains and close the doors. If the weather was rough the door closing might be left until the tug and barge reached calmer more sheltered water inside the Breakwater. The empty barge would be towed either to the Dockyard or to a mooring off Torpoint, ready to replace a loaded barge and so the cycle continued. The normal practice was to dump one barge every day. At times extra barges would be required to be moored alongside ships at anchor in the Hamoaze and the ship's ashes and refuse dumped straight in, and this would mean that there were extra barges to be towed out and dumped on some days. Often in the winter, the weather might be too rough to go out so loaded barges were taken to the moorings at Torpoint and when the weather improved, several barges would have to be towed out to sea to be dumped in one day. It will be apparent from the above description that in order to meet the contractual arrangements to

provide empty barges that Reynolds needed to own a very minimum of three barges, but in practice to allow for weather delays, repairs etc four or five were in use.

To revert to 1912, £2 was earned when the *Saxon* tried to pull the schooner *Red Rose* of Glasson Dock, off the beach at Torpoint. The schooner had been blown ashore in a gale, but the *Saxon*'s attempt was apparently unsuccessful as the schooner was not refloated until some months later, by George Treleaven's tug *Boarhound*, which was later to be owned by Reynolds. On 27 September the same year the hopper *Thames* sank alongside the Dockyard wall and was subsequently raised with the help of a Naval lifting lighter, and taken to Torpoint for repair.

1913 began with the purchase of another purpose built tug. The wooden built *Briton* arrived at Torpoint from Falmouth, purchased once again from William Rowe. The *Briton* was bigger being 68 feet long and had an engine developing 210 IHP. The *Briton* was comparatively new having been built in Falmouth by W. H. Lean in 1905 and this was reflected in the price of £1,750. Around this time Reynolds seems to have employed a professional mariner to manage the marine side of the business as a Captain George Andrews was in employment and was deemed important enough within the organisation to have his own business cards. The *Briton* did not have a very good first year. On 20 April she was used to tow a hopper out to dump for the first time with Captain Andrews in charge and on 1 May towed a barque from Plymouth to Par, her first (and possibly Reynolds' first) outside towing job. On the 2 July the *Briton* ran into a vessel named *Rescue*. This may have been either the

A hopper barge of similar vintage and size to the hopper barges used by W. J. Reynolds on the Dockyard refuse contract. This hopper barge was built in 1911, and is owned by the Laxey Towing Company Ltd in the Isle of Man.
F KISSACK

The BRITON with what appears to be a party of several, probably Reynolds', ladies on board.
W. J. REYNOLDS

locally owned schooner, *Rescue*, or another local tug named *Rescue* and owned by Fox and Co the shipping agents. It is possible that it was the latter vessel as long serving Reynolds' crew man, the late Reg Southard, recalled that even in the days after the Great War, when sailing ships were still plentiful, the tugs would sail at night out into the Sound and English Channel with no navigation lights exhibited to try to outwit the opposition and be first to find a lucrative tow, so collisions were far from unknown. What damage was caused to either vessel is not recorded. On 18 September the torpedo boat *108* was in collision with a hopper towed by the *Briton*. This torpedo boat was one of a class built by Thornycroft at Chiswick and was 160 feet long with a speed of 25 knots. A court of enquiry was held on the Devonport Base Ship *HMS Doris*, an Eclipse Class Cruiser, on 22 September. Less than a month later, on 3 October the *Briton* ran into the ferry (presumably the Torpoint chain ferry). Reynolds must have considered that this catalogue of accidents involving their best tug may have had something to do with her captain as George Andrews' employment was terminated the next day.

During 1913 Reynold bought a further hopper barge from a Mr Turner of Plymouth for the sum of £95 but the year ended badly when the collier *Rockwood*, belonging to William France Fenwick, collided with and sank the hopper barge *Tap* which was moored off Torpoint. Whilst the *Tap* was raised and repaired an iron hopper barge was hired from Pethick Bros of Plymouth who were railway and civil engineering contractors. It cost £32 for a month's hire.

W. J.'s wife Rebecca was also running her own business. She was the proprietor of a dress shop in East Cornwall House, Torpoint. The upper floor was occupied by the Town Council and on the ground floor were two shops of which Mrs Reynolds rented one. This property was destroyed by bombing during the Second World War. In February 1913 the well known Plymouth ship and barge owner, John Westcott, died, and in a newspaper report of the funeral, W. J. Reynolds is listed in the forefront of a long list of mourners, after the family, which indicates that after some 30 years in business he was regarded as a man of some considerable standing in the Plymouth community.

"BRITON" and "SAXON,"

Powerful Screw Tugs,

FOR HARBOUR AND SEA WORK.
USUAL TARIFF FOR TOWING.

Owner—W. J. REYNOLDS, Jun., Loch Lomond, Torpoint.

N.B.—All Towage Contracts are subject to the Condition that the Tug Owner shall not be answerable for any loss or damage which may happen to, or be occasioned by, the Vessel in tow.

Telephone 17 (Torpoint).   Captain G. ANDREWS.

Captain George Andrews' business card 1913.
JILL WILTSHIRE

The ALEXANDRA off St Mawes, when owned by the St Mawes Steam Tug & Passenger Company of Falmouth. She was purchased by Reynolds in 1919. ALAN KITTRIDGE COLLECTION

CHAPTER THREE

GROWTH AND CONSOLIDATION

Perhaps realising that war was inevitable, on 12 June 1914 Reynolds purchased another hopper barge, named *Jubilee*, for the sum of £300. It is not known who they bought her from but it may well have been the barge previously hired from Pethick Bros. The somewhat high price might indicate a modern well found vessel, however nine days after her purchase, the *Jubilee* sank whilst alongside the Dockyard wall. She was raised the next day, repaired and back in service by 26 June. The high purchase figure was more likely to have reflected monetary inflation with the prospect of war.

On 24 August 1914 an event occurred which could have had dire consequences for the Reynolds. The family had banked with a concern called the Naval Bank and on this date the bank suspended payment and ceased trading. The previous year in 1913 all the ships papers (official registration documents giving legal title to a vessel) had been lodged with the bank. This would only have been done to secure an overdraft or mortgage, probably to finance the purchase of the *Briton* and various barges. However, in the event it was quickly arranged to transfer the business to Lloyds Bank so possible financial embarrassment was avoided.

The outbreak of war in September 1914 had a marked effect on Plymouth. In 1914 there were nearly 10,000 civilian workers in Devonport Dockyard and this rose to 19,000 by 1918. Vast quantities of waste would be generated, requiring disposal. On the outbreak of war Reynolds were operating four tugs, the *Lorna*, *Mascotte*, *Saxon* and *Briton*, but in 1915 the *Saxon* was taken over by the War Office, and renamed for the duration of hostilities *AS 135*. It may be wondered why the War Office did not take the more powerful *Briton*, but perhaps Reynolds were able to argue that they needed a powerful seagoing tug to tow the hoppers to sea to dump, and so the *Briton* escaped Government service.

On 1 September 1914 Reynolds accepted, after negotiation, a rate increase for the Dockyard work. It would appear that the tugs and barges remained very busy during this period and no doubt long hours were worked by Reynolds' staff and the family. Apart from this, few incidents have been recorded during the war years. In 1915 the bay mare *Darby* with her cart fell into a hopper at the Dockyard wall with predictable results. On 24 March 1916 W. J. Reynolds had to travel to Bodmin. He appeared at the Central Appeal Tribunal to seek exemption from conscription to military service for two of his employees, Paul and

Groggett, presumably pleading that the men, as Reynolds' employees, were engaged on work vital to the war effort. The plea was successful, at least in the short term as they were each granted one month's exemption. One wonders whether they were later called up and with what result.

On the 2 April 1916 Reynolds purchased yet another un-named hopper barge from the Elford family of Oreston. The Elfords were the major shareholders in the Oreston and Turnchapel Steamboat Company, which ran an intensive ferry service between the villages of Oreston and Turnchapel, and Sutton Harbour in Plymouth, and owned quite a number of steamboats. This barge cost the Reynolds £220. On 8 August the same year Reynolds purchased a property, a terraced house, number 5 Gordon Terrace, Torpoint for £240 – this gives a good comparison as to the cost of shipping compared with property at the time.

1918 produced its share of minor troubles starting on 24 June when the *Saxon*'s boiler 'gave out'. She was towed to Willoughby's shipyard in Millbay Docks where the old boiler was lifted out by 1 July and a replacement fitted soon afterwards. On 22 July a Dockyard lighter the *YC22* crushed the hopper *Jubilee* at the Sea Wall and on 18 November the *Saxon* broke down again with a broken piston rod – as she was still on charter to the War Department at this time they probably had to meet the cost of the repairs. Another hopper barge, named *Yank*, was purchased and required some repairs and sheathing (doubling over the plating or planking with an extra layer of material) before being put into service for the first time on 21 November. This would suggest quite an old vessel. The war had produced a substantial increase in business for Reynolds and the family no doubt emerged at the end of hostilities in a very sound financial position. As far as can be traced, Wilfred and Fearnley were employed full time in the business during the war years, having joined their father. Of the other sons, Claude apparently remained working in the Dockyard but joined the family firm shortly afterwards, and during the war Arthur became a Major in the Royal Engineers.

In February 1919 W. J. and his son Wilfred travelled to Falmouth to inspect the tug *Alexandra*. This vessel had been built of steel in 1902 by Cox of Falmouth for the St Mawes Steam Tug and Passenger Company and had spent most of her time prior to the outbreak of war as a passenger steamer on the St Mawes to Falmouth ferry and running coastal excursions from Falmouth. During the war she too had been chartered by the War Department, as an examination vessel at Falmouth, and on her return was completely refurbished at Cox's. The *Alexandra* was 84 feet long, very fast, and had a 300 horse power triple expansion engine also built by Cox. Purchase was agreed, a deposit paid and the *Alexandra* arrived at Torpoint on 4 March 1919. Reynolds paid a staggering £4,180 for the tug, but it proved a good investment as she lasted well into the 1960s, outliving all the other Cox built passenger tugs of the River Fal, of which there were a number owned by different concerns. The price reflected war time inflation as much as the excellent condition of the *Alexandra*.

The tug was soon at work and her size and power enabled more long distance tows to be undertaken. During October the tug went to Fowey

and towed a dredger and hopper barge to the Great Western Railway's Millbay Docks where dredging was to be undertaken, and in the same month she towed one of the Torpoint floating bridges, always difficult tows, around the corner to Millbay Docks for repairs. Her first master was Dicky Grant and he once undertook a long and difficult tow with a disabled ship from Plymouth to Pembroke Dock, Milford Haven. The *Saxon* was returned from her charter in August 1919 but was taken on charter again by the Admiralty, for a month in 1920.

One of the few documents to survive regarding Reynolds is a sort of a rough purchase book which logs in date order various purchases and events. It records the purchases of tugs and barges, but also shows that there was a constant trade in cart horses, in fact there are far more entries relating to horses than vessels. The majority of the horses seem to have been bought in as fully grown animals. No doubt the Dockyard work was hard and like the hopper barges, Reynolds would have had to keep quite a number of 'spare' animals to ensure the continuity of service. When the mill pond at Carbeile was filled in, the original intention was to provide more grazing area for the horses, but eventually the ground was sold to become a sports field and remains to this day the home of Torpoint Athletic Football Club.

In about 1925 another major property was acquired. On the water front at Torpoint was the Patent Manure Works. This had ceased trading and Reynolds bought the works from the owner, the Pole Carew Estates. It came with its own small dock, Carew Wharf, and Reynolds established a coal merchants business, which quickly gained an important contract, to supply the coal to the Torpoint ferries (it may well have been the anticipation of this contract which prompted the purchase). Every Friday

ALEXANDRA was built by Cox of Falmouth in 1902, and was the first Reynolds' tug with a triple expansion engine. In this picture the former Falmouth passenger tug is moored off Torpoint.
W. J. REYNOLDS

Carew Wharf as it is today, once the buildings of the Torpoint and District General Supply Co Ltd.
ALAN KITTRIDGE

evening all the shore staff would be employed hauling coal down to the ferry slip and coaling up each ferry. Reynolds' own tugs would be coaled as well and they eventually developed a big domestic coal round which delivered household coal far and wide from Torpoint. They also started trading from here as agricultural merchants (it will be remembered that from the earliest days Reynolds would buy fresh produce from other farmers to sell on to the Navy, so this was a natural progression) and this business became known as the Torpoint and District General Supply Co. Local barges, schooners and later coasters used to berth at Carew Wharf and bring in cargoes of coal, building and agricultural supplies. Apart from the local barges often quite famous schooners such as the *Result* (which is still with us preserved at the Ulster Folk Museum, just outside Belfast) would bring in cargoes. Once the local dockers went on strike, when trying to discharge a lime cargo which had 'hardened up' on passage.

On the foreshore at Torpoint was an old rectangular stone dock known as the Ballast Pond, constructed originally for sailing ships to load or discharge ballast. This was also purchased by Reynolds and on the inner sheltered side, facing Torpoint, a grid was constructed so the under water parts of the various vessels could be maintained. A grid is a structure usually made of a number of large square timber baulks, these are fastened to the sea bed at right angles to a quay wall and are spaced 4 or 5 feet apart and usually about 2 feet high. A vessel would then be floated in at high water over the top of the timbers, and as the tide went out the vessel

28

would settle on the timbers and at low water could be painted or minor repairs could be made to the bottom of the vessel. The Ballast Pond remains to this day as Torpoint Yacht Harbour.

By this period, Carbeile Mill had been equipped as an engineering shop. In the early years the machinery, lathes and saws may well have been driven by the water wheel which originally drove the corn grinding machinery, and Reynolds employed shipwrights, blacksmiths, boilermakers and fitters who were engaged in keeping the fleet of vessels and the carts and machinery in good working order. Add to this the crews of the tugs *Saxon*, *Briton* and *Alexandra* (the *Mascotte* had been scrapped in 1919 when the *Saxon* was returned from war service), the barge crews, the staff at the coal merchants, the horsemen working the carts in the Dockyard and two or three staff looking after the horses and running the farm, it is hardly surprising that Reynolds were fast becoming the largest employer of civilian labour in Torpoint.

The ballast Pond, Torpoint, and the site of the grid, once owned by W. J. Reynolds and now the Torpoint Yacht Harbour.
ALAN KITTRIDGE

TREVOL towing a new Torpoint floating bridge from the builders, Philip & Sons. Leaving Dartmouth, 9 May 1931. W. J. REYNOLDS

CHAPTER FOUR

OPPORTUNITY AND EXPANSION

Although Reynolds were well established by the early 1920s, they did not undertake that much ordinary towage of ships (although they did some work in this field). The mainstay was the Dockyard contracts and the tugs would be busy moving barges about and towing them to sea to dump. Usually when the chain ferries at Torpoint and Saltash required to be towed for overhaul, Reynolds' tugs would be used in the intricate operation or removing one from the chains and replacing it with the spare ferry on each service before towing one away, sometimes to Willoughby's in Millbay Docks, or even to Philips at Dartmouth.

From the 1890s to 1920, the majority of the ship towage work in the Plymouth area was undertaken by a Plymouth man, George F. Treleaven; who operated a fleet of tugs known as the Hound Line. Treleaven was a coal merchant and he acquired a number of tugs; the little *Deerhound*, the larger *Wolfhound* and *Sleuthound* – the latter which he later sold to the South African Government; and two ex Belgian tugs, the *Leopold I* and *Leopold II* – both being named after successive Kings of the Belgians. The *Leopold I* had been built in 1881 and was bought by Treleaven in about 1905. She was a 72 feet tug of 180 IHP. At the same time the *Leopold II*, a 73 feet tug of originally 130 IHP, was purchased. It is thought that both tugs had been purchased from a scrap dealer, who had removed the engine and boiler from the *Leopold II* and Treleaven purchased only the hull, which the *Leopold I* towed to Plymouth. The *Leopold II* was then placed in the hands of Willoughby's at Millbay. A brand new boiler, built by Riley's of Stockton-on-Tees, was installed and a new compound engine of 200 IHP

BELOW LEFT:
G. F. Treleaven's
DEERHOUND,
pictured after being sold to T. R. Brown of Bristol.
AUTHOR'S
COLLECTION

BELOW RIGHT:
G. F. Treleaven's
SLEUTHOUND,
which was sold to South Africa.
AUTHOR'S
COLLECTION

The WOLFHOUND *being cut up at Sharpness.* MIKE NASH COLLECTION

fitted. This engine had been built as an exhibition engine by Willoughby's apprentices and it is said that during the tug's subsequent service at Plymouth, the engine never required any new brasses (crankshaft bearings) and the boiler never had a tube replaced. *Leopold II* on completion of her major refit was renamed *Boarhound*, but as far as can be traced the *Leopold I* remained with her original name. George Treleaven died on 11 February 1918 and for a time the tugs were run by his daughter. Prior to his demise he had already sold the *Deerhound* to Bristol, the *Wolfhound* to South Wales, and as recounted the *Sleuthound* to South Africa.

Reynolds grabbed the opportunity and in April 1920 purchased both the *Leopold I* and the *Boarhound* from Treleaven's executors. And, equally importantly took on the crews including Treleaven's senior tug master Captain William Daymond. On purchase the *Leopold I* was renamed *Scraesdon*, a local place name in Antony Parish. This allowed Reynolds to take on the majority of the ship towing work in the Port of Plymouth, Captain Daymond having good contacts with the Plymouth pilots. Treleaven had also held the contract with Trinity House to carry out the transfers of the lighthouse keepers on the Eddystone Lighthouse, 12 miles outside Plymouth, and this valuable contract was also taken over by Reynolds. William Daymond's son Stan, who also worked for Treleaven and then Reynolds, recalled many years later that when Treleaven died, Joe Haskell, the stevedore, approached his father with a view to buying the tugs and the Daymond's running them. However, for whatever reason, it was not to be and both the tugs and their crews joined Reynolds' instead.

The *Boarhound* was about 76 feet in overall length and was regarded by her various masters as a very handy vessel. On one occasion she was turned right around in the 83 feet wide entrance to Millbay Docks inner basin without touching the sides. This manoeuvre can be achieved with the wind in the right direction by what is known as 'backing and filling'. A conventional single screw tug with an open propeller will quarter or kick one way when going astern, the reason for this being known as transverse thrust where the bottom of the propeller being more deeply immersed than the top produces a sideways thrust as well as an ahead or astern thrust. This means that on a vessel with a right handed propeller, when going astern the stern of the tug will swing to port and the bow to starboard and the opposite if the propeller is left handed. In order to turn around in a very short space in a tug with a right hand propeller, the helm is put hard a starboard and the engine is run alternately full ahead then full astern and by doing this, especially if the wind can be placed on the tug's port side to assist the swing, a good tug can be turned in her own length and an experienced tug master will use this ability to place his tug in position for towing.

This expansion was probably the catalyst for the family deciding in 1926 to take on limited liability status. Up until this time they had simply traded as a sort of a loose family partnership but on 3 July 1926 W. J. Reynolds Limited was incorporated. The authorised share capital was £10,000 in £1 shares and the subscribers were Wilfred John Reynolds of Coryton House, Torpoint, an Engineer, Walter Fearnley Reynolds of Cambridge House, Torpoint, an Engineer, Arthur Basil Reynolds of 22 Tremayne Terrace, Torpoint, an Engineer, and Rebecca Martin Reynolds, of Loch Lomond, Torpoint, a married woman. Interestingly William John Reynolds, the founder does not appear amongst the subscribers, but as he would be 71 at this time he had probably decided to retire from taking an active role in the business and was content to legally leave things to his sons and wife, but he no doubt still had his say behind the scenes.

The first acquisition of the limited company occurred that year when the tug *Eagle* was purchased. The *Eagle* had been built in London in 1896 for the War Office and had spent her career based at Devonport, used mainly for target towing and moving ammunition and bunker barges about the Dockyard and servicing the forts on either side of Plymouth Sound. She was offered for sale by tender and purchased by Reynolds. One story, which cannot be verified, suggested that she was purchased at auction by Joe Haskell who sold her on to Reynolds. Whether this is true is certainly not reflected in the registration documents, but the story was told by a person who was involved with the tugs at the time and cannot be discounted. The *Eagle* was quite a small tug of 60 feet long with a 150 IHP compound engine. Reynolds immediately renamed the vessel *Wolsdon*, another local place name in Antony Parish. The *Wolsdon* had other stories told about her, one tale suggested that she crossed the Atlantic twice under her own steam, (which the tug would not have either the coal

The BOARHOUND, built 1882, ex LEOPOLD II originally named after Leopold II, King of the Belgians.
W. J. REYNOLDS

bunker or fresh water capacity to do); another suggested that the tug sailed to Gibraltar during the Great War, which is more than possible although no definitive confirmation of this can be found.

One of the early jobs for the *Wolsdon* was to assist with laying a new electricity cable across the River Tamar at Saltash. Reynolds' workshops modified one of the barges as a cable layer and the *Wolsdon* together with the larger *Briton* worked the cable across the river, one tug either side of the barge.

On incorporation, the ownership of all the tugs and barges was transferred into the name of the limited company and the brothers then took a gamble which paid off handsomely. During the Great War the Government had commissioned the building of a great variety of vessels, including many tugs. One of a number of classes of standard tugs, were known as HS tugs, some were single screw and some twin screw, and they were built to a standard design by a number of different builders. After the war many were sold off and in 1926 at least five of these HS tugs were lying for sale at Ramsgate. The tugs were the *HS28, HS29, HS30, HS31* and *HS35*. W. J. Reynolds Ltd purchased four of the five from a company named Crichton

Thompson & Co Ltd of London. All were 90 feet long single screw tugs with compound engines developing about 450 IHP. The tug in the best

The WOLSDON *built 1896, ex-* EAGLE, *raising steam and preparing for a job.*
PAUL RICHARDS

The BRITON (right) and WOLSDON with a barge, laying a new power cable across the River Tamar at Saltash. As well as the tug crews and men on the barge, there are at least two well dressed gentlemen, one on the foredeck of the BRITON and one on the foredeck of the barge, who are thought to be two of the Reynolds brothers. W. J. REYNOLDS

A closer view of the barge with cable laying gear fitted. DAVID MARTIN

The ANTONY ex-
HS29 leaving
Ramsgate Harbour
after purchase by
Reynolds in 1926.
DAVID MARTIN

BELOW LEFT:
The HS30 as the
MOUNT MANISTY
when in the
ownership of the
Manchester Ship
Canal Co.
Although purchased
by Reynolds in
1926 this tug and
her sister were
quickly resold and
never entered
Reynolds' active
fleet.
TED GRAY

BELOW RIGHT:
The HS31 as the
CADDISHEAD when
in the ownership of
the Manchester
Ship Canal Co.
TED GRAY

condition was the *HS29*, and Reynolds took this into the fleet and named her *Antony*. Two of the tugs *HS30* and *HS31* were almost immediately resold to the Manchester Ship Canal Company where they became the *Mount Manisty* and *Caddishead*. Reynolds towed the remaining tug to Dartmouth for refitting at Philips yard. What is not clear is which of the HS tugs the fourth tug was. There is some confusion over the registration. Several sources suggest that it was the *HS28* which was towed to Dartmouth and when this vessel entered service with Reynolds was renamed *Trevol* (another place name in Antony parish). However, both *Lloyds Register of Shipping* and the *Mercantile Navy Lists* show the *Trevol* as being built by Hawthorns of Leith, who built a single HS tug, *HS35*. The *HS28* was built by Philips of Dartmouth; so somewhere along the line the identities of these two vessels seems to have become mixed up. What is not in doubt is that the sale of the two to the Manchester Ship Canal paid for the purchase of all four tugs. This effectively meant that W. J. Reynolds Ltd had managed to acquire two modern powerful ship handling tugs, for nothing.

Some of the HS tugs, when built, were fitted with automatic towing winches, and towing was undertaken from the winch which had a large drum on which was wound a wire rope. This was an American innovation and most North American tugs operated in this way but it was quite

TREVOL with grey hull and original wheelhouse, towing a freighter out of Millbay inner basin.
W. J. REYNOLDS

unusual in Britain. Normally British tugs towed off a towing hook. Certainly the *Trevol* was fitted with a towing winch and there are several photographs of the tug towing off the winch.

By the start of 1927 the tug fleet consisted of the *Antony*, *Trevol*, *Alexandra*, *Briton*, *Saxon*, *Wolsdon*, *Boarhound* and *Scraesdon*; with a similar number of barges. However, within two years the *Saxon* and *Scraesdon* were taken out of service and scrapped. They probably went out of use when the newer larger tugs arrived and it became the habit of W. J. Reynolds Ltd to move redundant tugs to the ballast pond where they were stripped of anything useful, non ferrous material, boiler fittings, ships wheels, compasses, bells etc which would be stored for possible further use or sold at a better price, until eventually only the hull and boilers were sold to a local shipbreaker.

Crew of the BRITON c.1925. The master, Captain Sam Bradford, is the middle figure of the three on deck.
D BRADFORD

The tugs were all moored on the 'trot'. This is a term for a line of vessels moored afloat. In Reynolds' case, a massive anchor chain with huge links, thought to have originally come from a large warship, was laid on the riverbed on the upstream side of the chain ferries. Each end was held by a very substantial sinker block weighing several tons. At intervals along this 'ground chain' as it was known, slightly smaller chains would be shackled on, leading up to a steel cylindrical buoy with a large ring on top. The buoy would hold the chain up when the tug was away at work and each tug had on the foredeck a length of chain which ended in a large hook. When mooring up the hook would be passed through the eye on the buoy and the chain hauled tight on the anchor windlass, lifting the buoy out of the water and so maintaining tension on the hook to prevent it jumping out. By using this method the tugs could get underway quickly in an emergency.

All the quay walls at Torpoint dried out at low water, so if the tugs had been left alongside Carew Wharf or the Ballast Pond, at low water they would be sitting on the bottom and unable to move. By mooring on the 'trot' the tugs were afloat at all states of the tide and therefore always available for service. Each tug had the use of a large wooden clinker built rowing boat kept at the ferry slip, which would be used by the crew to board the tug, and when the tug sailed the rowing boat would be moored to the buoy and retrieved when the tug returned.

The next tug to arrive at Torpoint was a large wooden vessel, the *Cruden Bay*. This tug had been built in Anstruther as a fish carrier in 1899 and had a compound engine of 210 IHP. The vessel came from the Fowey Tug Company but the registration papers record that on 3 July 1928, the registration was closed, the vessel having been broken up, on advice from the owners, the Fowey Tug and Salvage Co. In other words, the vessel was never registered in Reynolds ownership. That the *Cruden Bay* came to Torpoint is not in doubt, as her remains lay on the foreshore well into the 1950s, and when the stripping had finally been completed, the lower part of the hull was towed around to Carbeile Creek where it was beached and remained a feature until at least the early 1990s. Some sources show the vessel as being owned officially by Reynolds, but the probability is that this tug was purchased cheaply for spares, or simply to keep the men employed in breaking the vessel up and recovering any scrap available for onward sale. In any case the final entry in the registration papers for 1928 indicating that the *Cruden Bay* had been broken up was somewhat premature, by nearly 70 years.

In 1928 the furnaces in the *Briton*'s boiler were getting thin, so Reynolds' own men removed the starboard furnace and fitted a new one, and the following year the port furnace was similarly replaced. Also in 1928 Reynolds sold the *Antony*, one of the two HS tugs, a good price being obtained from the Shipowners Towage Syndicate at Antwerp, where the tug was renamed *Cooperator*. Apart from the other HS tugs which were bought and re-sold without entering Reynolds' active fleet, the *Antony* was the only tug that was sold out of the fleet for further service. The *Antony* was probably sold in preference to the *Trevol* because the latter tug was fitted with a steam towing winch, which would certainly be useful when towing the hoppers out to dump. The towing gear could be lengthened or shortened in by one man operating the winch instead of most of the crew handling heavy hawsers on deck. The *Antony* was fitted with the more usual standard towing hook. Every other tug that Reynolds purchased ended up finishing their working lives with the firm to be broken up.

Around this period, photographs show that the colour scheme of the tugs changed. Originally the hulls had been painted black but for a time in the inter war period the hulls from the waterline to deck level were painted battleship grey. Given the Dockyard refuse contract this is not surprising and one possibly apocryphal tale suggested that the nickname 'Tacky' Reynolds came from this colour change. The Navy had disposed of large numbers of redundant tins of grey paint, and it is said that rather than dumping the paint at sea, Reynolds saved them and economically used the paint on the hulls of the tugs. However, the paint did not dry well, the Navy had discarded the paint because it had a problem – when applied it remained 'tacky' for a long time. However, another suggestion has been that W. J. Reynolds was very interested in his horses and liked them to be well turned out when at work, with good clean harnesses, or 'tack' as it is sometimes known in the equine world.

Depositing refuse at sea is today frowned upon but in earlier times the sea was regarded as a legitimate dumping ground. Wilfred Reynolds' (styled W. J. Reynolds, Jun.) business card from the early 1920s indicates that they were Government Contractors, Tug and Lighter Owners, Engineers and Agents, and had available Channel or Harbour Tugs fitted with salvage pumps, Hoppers and Lighters available for hire and Oil Fuel Residue deposited at sea. How the oil fuel residue was dumped is not clear. It is not thought that Reynolds owned any tank barges at this time, more likely the residue was barrelled and dumped by means of the ordinary hopper barges. Whatever the case, one can imagine the outcry if such a method of disposal was suggested today.

W. J. Reynolds Ltd was now undertaking all sorts of towage work. The *Alexandra* and *Boarhound* were tasked to tow a partly dismantled naval sloop from Plymouth to ship breakers at Salcombe. After delivering the sloop both tugs made their way back to Torpoint at a steady 8 knots, this being the usual speed of the *Boarhound*. The *Alexandra*, commanded by Captain Sam Bradford, was considerably faster but held back, but the story is told that Dick Bradford, the engineer on the *Alexandra* couldn't resist letting the 'Alex' run ahead and then slow down to allow the *Boarhound* to catch up. Captain William Daymond on the *Boarhound* was not too bothered but Harry the

W. J. Reynolds, Jnr, (Wilfred Reynolds) business card from the 1920s
JILL WILTSHIRE

Boarhound's engineer was not so pleased. As darkness approached he got some more help in the engine room, built up a full head of steam and ran the *Boarhound*'s engine flat out and for once beat the *Alexandra*.

Another job was the re-floating of the coaster *Olivene* which had run aground between Salcombe and Prawle Point. The casualty was inside a reef which was covered at high tide and the *Boarhound* was dispatched to try and tow the ship off. The first attempt was unsuccessful so the *Wolsdon* was sent to assist. The weather was perfect and the *Boarhound* had remained with the *Olivene* inside the reef at low water. When the *Wolsdon* neared, the reef had covered and her crew seemed unaware of the exact location of the outlying rocks, only the crew of the *Boarhound* waving and shouting prevented the *Wolsdon* from becoming a casualty. Eventually the *Olivene* was re-floated by the two tugs. The *Boarhound* and *Wolsdon* were probably used as opposed to the bigger more powerful tugs, as they were the tugs with the least draft and could get in closer to the grounded ship.

In November 1928 the *Boarhound* encountered a coaster the *Kentish Coast*, in ballast and trying to proceed in the teeth of a severe south west gale. A tow was offered but the offer ignored, which proved to be a false economy for the *Kentish Coast* as the steamer was eventually blown ashore in Jennycliff Bay. She was later pulled clear by a large Dockyard tug with Reynolds' tugs assisting.

Around 1929 a cinema film entitled *Q Ships* was being made at Plymouth. The film company had acquired an obsolete submarine which was being towed to various locations between the Breakwater and the

Towing a 'wooden wall' in Sutton Pool with three tugs, TREVOL ahead, ALEXANDRA alongside, and SCRAESDON astern.
DAVID MARTIN

Eddystone Rocks. Usually the *Trevol* was towing and the *Boarhound* followed with a camera crew on board, sometimes filming from the top of her diminutive wheelhouse. At night the submarine was moored off Drake's Island until one Sunday evening the moorings parted in a gale and the submarine was blown ashore. However, when the gale abated the tugs were able to re-float the submarine which luckily had suffered very little damage.

1930 saw yet more salvage work, In September the 4,950 ton steamer *Umberleigh* bound from Barry to Antwerp in ballast was blown ashore in a fierce gale at Bovisand Bay. In difficult conditions the ship was pulled free by the *Boarhound*, Captain Stan Daymond; *Trevol*, Captain William Daymond and *Alexandra*, Captain Fearnley Reynolds. The *Boarhound* had actually been tasked to tow a cable ship out of the inner basin at Millbay Docks, but because of the severe weather conditions the Dockmaster decided he did not want to open the dock gates, so the *Boarhound* took the opportunity to assist with the salvage. The large twin screw Admiralty Dockyard tug *Retort* was also in attendance, but had the misfortune to get a rope entangled in one of her propellers. W. J. Reynolds were subsequently awarded £2,200 for the salvage, the Dockyard award being £650. Each of the respective Reynolds' tug masters received their share of £17, which although does not seem much today, was probably two or three week's wages then.

According to the hand written purchase diary, on 26 February 1931 Reynolds purchased a tug called *Hasty*. According to Claude Reynolds

The COMMONWEALTH as purchased. This photograph was thought to be taken by Wilfred and Fearnley Reynolds when they travelled to Bristol to inspect the tug; the photo is taken at the King Edward Lock at Avonmouth.
W. J. REYNOLDS

daughter the *Hasty* was not a tug but an ex-mining vessel and was originally operated by the Royal Engineers for laying mines in the Sound. The *Hasty* was taken over by the Royal Navy and Reynolds bought the vessel just to dismantle for spares and scrap. The *Hasty* was built by Hawthorns of Leith in 1891 as the *Napier of Magdala*, later was renamed *Linnet* and finally *Hasty*. She was 80 feet long with a beam of 18 feet and a gross tonnage of 177.

Around the same period Reynolds purchased a fifth HS tug (probably *HS35*) which had been for sale at Ramsgate in 1926. The tug was apparently not taken into the Reynolds' fleet and was thought to have been resold, but details have proved elusive. In December the same year, another hopper barge was acquired, the *Claretta*, from Plymouth Corporation.

In 1934 the brothers obviously felt that another more powerful tug was needed. At this time, following the sale of the *Antony* to Belgium, and with ships becoming larger, the *Trevol* was the only powerful member of the fleet. Wilfred and Fearnley travelled to Bristol and examined afloat the tug *Commonwealth*, which was owned by Sydney Roberts' Commonwealth Steam Tug Company. The *Commonwealth* was in fact the first tug Sydney Roberts had purchased in his own right after falling out with his brothers after the death of their father, Bristol tug owner Charles Roberts. Sydney named his new company after his first tug. The *Commonwealth* was a 90 feet tug built in 1902 by Hepple and Co of South Shields for the Empire Towing Co of Gravesend. Her compound engine developed 585 IHP. She was noted for salvage work in her early days and was fully equipped with large salvage pumps. Early in her career she successfully salvaged the *SS Flora* which was in a sinking condition having been in a collision in the Thames. The brothers were suitably impressed and arranged for the tug to be dried out on the grid iron at the Cumberland Basin at the Bristol City Docks. They

The mining vessel (mine layer) HASTY, bought from the Admiralty in 1931. Never used by Reynolds she was possibly purchased for spares. Her ultimate fate is unknown but she was probably broken up in the 1930s.
AUTHOR'S COLLECTION

42

found the hull to be in excellent condition and a deal to purchase was concluded at a price of £1,700. This was less than half the price paid for the *Alexandra* in 1919, for a tug of nearly double the power; the *Commonwealth* arrived on the Tamar on 30 October 1934 and was renamed *Antony* (2)

Another much smaller vessel was purchased at this time. The *Vussel* was a 42 feet long wooden 12 oared rowing gig reputedly built in Gibraltar for use on a battleship. Reynolds' Carbeile Mill engineering works was well equipped and the *Vussel* was initially used as a floating workshop. The hull was of double diagonal teak planking, and Reynolds fitted an electric arc welding plant and oxy acetelene cutting gear aboard the boat. At this time electric arc welding was pretty much in its infancy as far as ship repairing was concerned, and having a floating plant allowed repairs to be carried out to vessels lying afloat. It was certainly 'state of the art' at the time. Whether the boat was named *Vussel* when purchased or whether given this name by Reynolds (and if so after what?) is not known.

Apart from ships trading to the various commercial docks, Millbay, Sutton Harbour, Cattedown Wharfs and Victoria Wharfs, Plymouth was booming as a port of call for Atlantic passenger liners. Liners would call at Plymouth and passengers and mails would be landed and taken to Bristol or London by express trains, making a considerable saving in time against staying on board until Southampton (*via* Cherbourg or Le Havre). Passengers could also board at Plymouth on outward voyages. To handle this traffic the owners of Millbay Docks, the Great Western Railway, had built up a fleet of passenger tenders. As the majority of the liners were too big to be accommodated alongside any of the commercial docks they anchored in Plymouth Sound, the passengers being landed by the tenders. When the ships were arriving or leaving, the liners often required the

The ANTONY (2), *ex-*COMMONWEALTH *alongside a ship in the Sound, photograph taken from the bridge of the* TREVOL

DAVID MARTIN

assistance of Reynolds' tugs to swing and guide them out to sea, and also often to carry 'odds and sods', engine spares, ships stores' etc out to the anchored ships. In August 1935 Reynolds' tugs were hired to recover and return an anchor to the French liner *Normandie*, which had lost one in Cawsand Bay. In order to do this Reynolds' hired a lifting lighter *YC23* from the Admiralty and the *Normandie*'s anchor was successfully returned to the ship.

Just under a year after buying the *Antony* (2), Arthur and Fearnley Reynolds travelled to Penzance, on 22 August 1935, and inspected a hopper barge, the *FHC No 2*. This barge belonged to Fowey Harbour Commissioners, but was surplus to requirements and had been chartered for a dredging job by the James Towing and Dredging Co of Southampton. The contract having been completed the barge was laid up at Penzance and the brothers agreed to purchase it for £150, which suggests that it was in pretty poor condition. While in Penzance they saw a tug belonging to James, also laid up at the completion of the dredging contract – the *Bahia* (always pronounced BAYA in Torpoint). Arrangements were made with the James Towing and Dredging Co and they returned to Penzance on 28 August, when a representative opened up the tug for inspection and trial, after which a purchase was agreed at £550. The *Bahia* was smaller than the *Commonwealth*, being about 80 feet long with a compound engine of 350 IHP. The tug had been built by Day Summers and Co at Southampton in 1907 for Wilson, Sons & Co of London for service in Brazil – hence the Portuguese name. Whether the tug ever went to Brazil is unclear, but it would seem unlikely, as such a long ocean

passage made the chances of a small vessel returning to England seem remote. Between 1923 and 1930 the *Bahia* had been owned by Captain Stephen Portus of Garston on the River Mersey. Over the years Captain Portus, who was an enterprising dock pilot and also employed the boatmen at Garston, owned and operated a number of tugs, which he usually managed to sell on at a profit.

One former Reynolds employee who, although he did not personally sail on the *Bahia*, sailed with men who did, reported that the tug was not liked by the crews. When towing a ship, the *Bahia* had a tendency to list over at an alarming angle when the tow rope was out on the beam. All tugs list when the rope is out at a 90 degree angle to the tug and in a conventional screw tug, this can become a dangerous situation as the tug can be 'girted,' i.e. pulled over so far sideways that the tug capsizes. Many tugs have been lost this way, but some tugs were (and are, in the author's experience), more prone to listing than others. One of the *Bahia*'s former owners, the aforementioned Captain Portus lost his life in one of his later tugs, the *Toxteth*, which was girted and capsized when on the stern of a ship leaving the Brunswick Lock at Liverpool in 1947, drowning most of the crew.

One thing in the *Bahia*'s favour was her speed. Her long narrow hull no doubt helped her in this, and on one occasion the *Bahia* was said to have made the passage between Millbay Docks and the Eddystone, a distance of just under 13 miles, in 55 minutes. Why she did this however, is something of a mystery, as normally when doing the Eddystone relief a rowing boat was towed astern (as will be explained in a later chapter) which meant that the tug had to proceed fairly cautiously so as not to swamp the rowing boat.

The BAHIA – the Portuguese named tug that was originally destined for service in Brazil. Pictures at Torpoint during W. J. Reynolds ownership with a wheelhouse replacing the open bridge.
W. J. REYNOLDS

The ALEXANDRA (left) and TREVOL getting ready to pull the famous HERZOGIN CECILIE off the rocks at Soar Mill Cove on 19 June 1936. Both tugs are lying head to tide, with tow ropes connected, probably with the engines running slow ahead to keep on station whilst waiting for the combination of a rising tide and a barrage of motor pumps on board the ship to float her free from the rocks. The tugs then turned to port, moved to a position slightly fine of the starboard bow of the ship and pulled at full power.
AALANDS MARITIME MUSEUM

CHAPTER FIVE

THE OLD ORDER CHANGETH

On 24 November 1936 William John Reynolds died. He was a man of drive and enterprise who was not afraid to take a chance on business opportunities and these usually paid off. He was an astute businessman, who apparently liked his horses and boats. According to family tradition he would go 'seeking' in his tugs in the early days, seeking being tugs proceeding to sea to try and find a sailing ship in need of a tow, but it is not thought that he usually sailed in command of these vessels, preferring to employ professional mariners. He liked to buy things second hand, a tradition continued by his sons and grandsons, but he could identify a good deal, and he was certainly well thought of by the inhabitants of Torpoint and those involved in marine and agricultural matters in the surrounding area. Certainly at the time of his death the business he founded was the largest employer of civilian labour in Torpoint. In earlier times he rode around in a pony and trap, and employed a trap boy to drive. If he went afloat in any of his tugs he expected the trap to be ready at a given time on his return, and any tardiness on the part of the trap boy was likely to result in a severe admonishment or even dismissal.

W. J. Reynolds'
obituary in the
CORNISH TIMES,
27 November
1936.
AUTHORS
COLLECTION

W. J. Reynolds died at the home of his son Claude, at 2 Albert Terrace Torpoint. His obituary records that on the occasion of his golden wedding in 1928, he received a message from King George V and he also received the thanks of the Admiralty for his special services during the Great War. Unfortunately the newspaper does not elaborate on what these special services were, but they were no doubt connected with extra work undertaken at the Dockyards. It also mentions that he was a founder member of the Carew Masonic Lodge and had been a member of the Good Templar Lodge since 1871. The report of his funeral gives a very extensive list of mourners indicating his standing, and the pall bearers were six Reynolds' staff members, Messrs H. Pearce, C. Hanslip, S. Parnell, W. Seeley, R. Skinner and L. Butson.

MR. W. J. REYNOLDS, TORPOINT.

The death on Tuesday of Mr. William John Reynolds, of Loch Lomond, Torpoint, deprives the town of a prominent resident. Born in 1854, Mr. Reynolds since the age of nine, had lived in Torpoint, and for 50 years was a Government contractor. At the outset he joined with his father in the removal of refuse from H.M. ships and dockyard by sailing and rowing boats, but later steam tugs and lighters were brought into service. Mr. Reynolds, by meeting officers and crews of warships of all nations visiting the port, collected many interesting reminiscences, which he delighted to relate.

On the occasion of his golden wedding in 1928, he received a message from King George, and he received the thanks of the Admiralty for special services during the Great War.

Mr. Reynolds had not served, as did his two brothers, on the Urban Council, but for several years was a member of the Board of Guardians. He was a founder of Carew Masonic Lodge, and was also a charter member of the Good Templar Lodge, with which he had been associated since 1871.

He leaves a widow, four sons, and a daughter.

A poor quality but none the less interesting picture of the ALEXANDRA and TREVOL manoeuvring the HERZOGIN CECILIE into position in Starhole Bay, Salcombe. The stern of the ALEXANDRA can be seen in the bottom left of the picture towing from the stern of the ship. Water from the numerous pumps can be seen discharging at several locations along the starboard side of the ship.
AALANDS MARITIME MUSEUM

In 1936, some months before his death, the tugs were engaged in at least two salvage jobs, the first of which made headlines not only in local papers but in the national and international press as well. On 25 April the famous four masted barque *Herzogin Cecilie* hit the Ham Stone rock at Soar Mill Cove near Bolt Head. The ship was commanded by Captain Sven Erikson who had his wife Pamela on board with him, and the vessel was part of the then famous fleet of square rigged sailing ships owned by Gustav Erikson of Marieham in the Aaland Islands.

The *Herzogin Cecilie* had been built to the highest standards as a cadet ship, and had been launched in Bremerhaven in 1902. At the time of her grounding the ship was carrying a cargo of over 4,000 tons of grain from Australia and had called, as was usual, at Falmouth for orders the previous day. On her arrival at Falmouth the ship had been arrested by the Admiralty Marshall as the result of a claim made regarding a collision the ship had been in prior to sailing to Australia, but a bond was quickly posted and the ship released to sail for her discharge port of Ipswich. In the early hours of the morning in fog the ship hit an outlying rock and the anchors were let go but the ship swung and finished up with her stern ashore. Word was sent for a tug from Plymouth and it is thought that the first tug on the scene was the *Briton*, but the master probably decided that his vessel was not powerful enough for the job. Shortly afterwards a large German salvage tug, the *Seafalke*, at the time one of the most powerful and best equipped salvage tugs in the world, arrived. Her highly experienced German master quickly decided that if acting under a standard Lloyds no cure no pay salvage agreement, that the costs and efforts involved in re-floating the *Herzogin Cecilie* would not be economically viable, and so the *Seafalke* left the scene. Captain Erikson then began methodically to discharge the cargo into sailing barges brought alongside at high water, a party of Cambridge University students volunteering to help with this work. Although the ship was leaking she was still basically intact.

On 10 June, with much cargo removed, and a barrage of salvage pumps running on board the stricken vessel, Reynolds sent the *Trevol* and *Alexandra* to attempt to re-float the ship, but although they pulled at full power, over the high water period, the ship did not move. Nine days later on a higher tide and with more pumps on deck the same tugs made a

48

further attempt, this time successfully and the *Herzogin Cecilie* was again afloat. The preferred plan had been to tow the ship into the sheltered waters of Salcombe, but the local authority was nervous about the stink from the rotting grain still aboard the ship affecting the holiday season and permission to bring the ship in was refused. However, permission was granted to beach the *Herzogin Cecilie* in Starhole Bay, a large fairly sheltered sandy inlet nearer Salcombe, where it was hoped that the remainder of the cargo could be discharged and some temporary repairs made to make the ship sea worthy enough to be towed to a dry dock for repair. The decision not to tow the ship straight to Plymouth or Falmouth was sensible and dictated by circumstance. The ship was only being kept afloat by means of the pumps, and any pump failure or increase in leakage might have caused the ship to sink under tow. No doubt the harbour authorities at both these ports would not have been very keen to allow the vessel to enter their respective fairways which, if the ship sank, could be blocked. This then could result in the sunken vessel becoming a major practical problem to the harbour authorities, on whom the job of removing the resultant wreck would have fallen, at considerable cost.

The *Trevol* and *Alexandra* successfully towed the ship the three miles from Soar Mill Cove to Starhole Bay, both tugs towing ahead of the ship. On arrival off Starhole Bay the *Alexandra* slipped her tow from the bow and took a line from the stern of the ship, and the *Trevol* moved to tow from a position just aft of amidships on the starboard side, and the tugs then towed the *Herzogin Cecilie* stern first into the bay so the ship was facing seaward, the best position to withstand any strong winds and seas. As far as Reynolds was concerned the operation was a great success, and Reynolds got paid. The salvage had been financed by a naval officer, Lieutenant Hudson, who at the time wished to remain anonymous. Although the re-floating and towing operation was successful, unknown to anybody, the sand at Starhole Bay covered a ridge of rock, and in the ensuing weeks the ship settled into the sand and eventually broke her back on the rocky ridge. This once fine vessel was partially dismantled where she lay and apparently her remains can sometimes be seen to this day.

The second salvage job that summer occurred on 23 September when the motor schooner *Amazon* was towed off the rocks in Cawsand Bay and delivered to the Lucas boatyard in the Cattewater for repairs. That she was repaired is quite surprising as the 66 feet long wooden *Amazon* had been built in Jersey in 1866 and was 70 years old. At the time of her stranding she was owned by Oscar Harris of Par.

Over a year elapsed before the next salvage job. The motor coaster *Sagacity* was a fairly new ship having been launched in May 1935. This 490 gross ton vessel was 153 feet long and powered by a Newbury 5 cylinder diesel engine. Not withstanding her recent construction, on 18 November 1937 the *Sagacity* broke down of Prawle Point, and the *Trevol* put to sea, connected a tow and successfully towed her to Plymouth for repairs. A salvage award of £800 ensued.

The Reynolds brothers decided that another tug was needed, probably

The LORD BERESFORD as built with a long North American style deck house and steam towing winch immediately aft of the deckhouse. MIKE DOHERTY COLLECTION

with a view to replacing the wooden *Briton,* which was by this time 32 years old, and it will be remembered that her boiler required extensive work in 1928/29. Arthur and Fearnley travelled to Bristol to meet Sydney Roberts and inspected two of his tugs, the *Mercia* and *Wolfhound,* the latter having begun her career at Plymouth when owned by G. F. Treleaven. They were not impressed however and on 3 April 1938 travelled to Great Yarmouth to inspect the tug *Tactful,* which at this time was owned by the Great Yarmouth Steam Tug Company Ltd. After a thorough inspection

The TACTFUL with the wheelhouse removed and open bridge towing two Thames sailing barges out of Great Yarmouth Harbour in 1934. MARITIME PHOTO LIBRARY

The TACTFUL *at Torpoint with wheelhouse re-instated.*
W. J. REYNOLDS

and trials, a deposit was paid on 5 April and the tug arrived at Torpoint on the 11th, being sailed from Yarmouth by her Yarmouth crew.

The *Tactful* was a 75 feet long tug built in 1909 by J. Fullerton of Paisley with a compound engine of 400 IHP. Her first owners were the Maritime Dredging and Construction Co Ltd of St Johns, New Brunswick, Canada, and she was originally named *Lord Beresford*. As built she had a long North American style deck house and a steam towing winch mounted on the after deck aft of the deckhouse. The tug re-crossed the Atlantic during the Great War when she was purchased by the War Department and subsequently had several UK owners. At some stage, certainly by the time she was at Great Yarmouth, her long deck house was cut back, the towing winch removed, and the more usual British style towing hook fitted. The *Tactful* was probably too expensive in capital terms for the work on offer at Great Yarmouth. Most of the work consisted of towing sailing fishing vessels and Thames spritsail barges in and out of the harbour, and there were still some very old paddle tugs operating at Yarmouth, along with a modern screw tug, the *George Jewson,* operated by the Port and Haven Commissioners.

On one occasion the *Tactful* failed to live up to her name. In October 1937 she put to sea to offer a tow to the sailing barge *Audrey*, which was anchored sheltering from a gale in Yarmouth Roads. When coming close she hit the bowsprit of the barge, bringing down some of the rigging and furled sails which went over the side. The waterlogged sails, pulled by the

The launch of a Mosquito class sailing yacht at Torpoint in the late 1930s. The Reynolds family supported many local sporting and charitable organisations and were instrumental with others in founding the Torpoint Mosquito Sailing Club, still very active today. The picture is taken pretty much where the present sailing club premises are situated. In the background can be seen the buildings of the Torpoint and District General Supply Company at Carew Wharf and the tug BOARHOUND *is berthed in the small dock used to import supplies of coal and building materials for the supply company.* DAVID MARTIN

currents, caused the anchor to drag – so the *Tactful* then 'had' to tow the barge in.

On 18 November 1938, the *Bahia* was damaged in a collision at Bull Point, the Navy's ammunition depot just below Saltash. What she was in collision with has not been recorded but Arthur Reynolds went across to survey the damage together with Reynolds' foreman shipwright Joe Butson. The damage could not have been too serious because exactly a week later the steam coaster *Jellicoe Rose* went ashore in Jennycliff Bay, and was towed off by the *Alexandra* and *Bahia* with the *Antony* and *Trevol* in attendance. The *Jellicoe Rose* was a 220 feet long steamship owned by Richard Hughes of Liverpool and had been built in 1920.

One of a number of long serving employees, Eric Martin joined the firm as an apprentice engine fitter and turner in 1937. During his first year his wages were 4 shillings a week rising to 14 shillings in the sixth and final year of his apprenticeship. Eric Martin remained with the firm as engineer, latterly on the *Antony*, until the end and then joined Cory's as engineer, working until he died in 1981 giving nearly 45 years service on tugs in Plymouth.

CHAPTER SIX

SECOND WORLD WAR

The build up to war must have been more than apparent to Reynolds, with ever increasing work from the Naval Dockyard. Although the towage of naval ships was usually the preserve of Naval and Dockyard tugs, at times these were so hard pressed that Reynolds' tugs would also operate within the Dockyard.

Just over a week before war was declared on 3 September 1939, the Ministry of War Transport activated a dormant charter on the *Briton*. It has been said that the *Briton* was, by this time, laid up at the Ballast Pond at Torpoint and was leaking to the extent of being almost tidal. However, Reynolds' shipwrights got to work and the *Briton* was soon able to undertake the charter, which fortuitously for Reynolds, lasted right through the war until 1946. Obviously realising that there would be much extra work in the Dockyard, Arthur and Fearnley travelled to Greenwich in November and inspected a hopper barge the *Clearwell*,

Scene at Torpoint on the day before 'D' Day with American infantry waiting to embark on the circling landing craft. To the top right of the picture can be seen the BOARHOUND, returning from dumping with an empty hopper barge breasted up alongside.
AUTHOR'S COLLECTION

which they purchased for £950. The next month the tug *Tactful* was taken over by the Admiralty and she remained on charter until July 1940 when she was returned. Reynolds did not have her back for long as the War Office took her on charter in February 1941 and she remained on Government service until 1946.

By the outbreak of war, Claude Reynolds had joined the family business and he ran the Torpoint and District General Supply Co, which had expanded greatly, branching out into building supplies as well trading in coal and agricultural supplies.

On 20 March 1941 the *Boarhound* was moored in Millbay Docks. It had been the custom to base a tug there on a more or less permanent basis to handle the busy traffic. Also, moored close to the *Boarhound*, was a barge, a French tug, the large Southampton tug *Sir Bevois* – which had been posted to assist at Plymouth at the start of the war, and a small freighter the *Mari II*. During the blitz of that night, the barge was hit by incendiary bombs, which luckily burnt themselves out, but the *Sir Bevois* was hit by a high explosive bomb which sunk her and the French tug, killing all the crew members of both vessels. The *Mari II* was lifted partially onto the quay by the blast and sank when she fell back into the water. Amazingly the old *Boarhound* stayed afloat, although her starboard side was peppered with shrapnel holes and many rivets were shaken loose. When the bombing had ceased, Captain Stan Daymond and his crew, returned to Millbay to find the *Boarhound* still there, and they managed to raise steam, start

Captain Stan Bradford at the wheel of the ANTONY, *he was in command of this tug during the war and for many years.*
DAVID BRADFORD

the pumps and limp back to Torpoint. The *Boarhound* was quickly repaired and returned to service. The sunken wrecks lay at Millbay for some time but the berths were needed for American troopships and the vessels were all raised, with some difficulty. The *Boarhound* returned to supply steam from her boiler to drive the salvage pumps. The French tug and the *Sir Bevois* came up without too much difficulty, and were scrapped, but the *Mari II* nearly capsized on the first attempt and was allowed to sink again. An American salvage officer was in charge and on the second attempt the freighter came up, although at one stage it looked

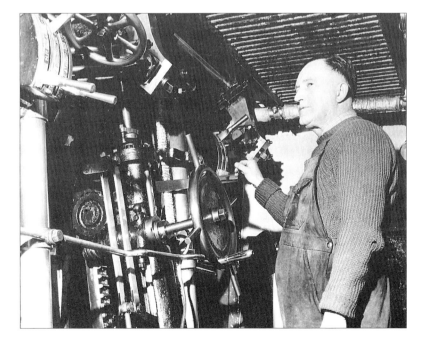

The ANTONY's *engine room with engineer Reg Butson at the controls.*
DAVID MARTIN

Steve Hannaford was mate on the ANTONY *during the war until promoted to master in 1947.*
GILL FERGUSON

as though the ship would capsize on top of the *Boarhound*, such a severe list did it develop.

Captain Stan Bradford was in command of the *Antony* for most of the war, and he recalled that the larger tugs were often handling a dozen ships a day, especially when the American troopships started arriving after 1942. A surviving crew list for the *Antony* for the second half of 1940 (see appendix) shows the tug to have a large crew of eight, probably extra crew were employed because of the long hours being worked and the fact that the *Antony*, *Trevol* and *Alexandra* were fitted with Lewis guns for protection, these being the tugs usually towing the hoppers out to sea to dump. On more than one occasion, the crew of the *Alexandra* were reputed to have observed the periscopes of enemy submarines but the tugs and barges were never attacked; possibly they were considered too small to waste a torpedo on, and too close to Plymouth to risk a surface attack.

Apart from the damage to the *Boarhound*, the Reynolds' fleet seemed to come through the war practically unscathed, although there were many difficulties for the horsemen with their charges working in the Dockyard, and the ferries still had to be coaled every Friday to keep the service going.

On 22 January 1944 the hopper barge *Yank* sank in No 5 basin at the Dockyard, she was raised by 30 January and towed to Torpoint for repair. Less than three weeks later the hopper barge *Tap* sank alongside the battleship HMS *Anson*, but was raised and repaired.

A large American Liberty Ship, the *James Egan Lane*, proceeding in convoy, was torpedoed near the Eddystone on 12 March 1945. The crew were taken off and the ship was taken in tow by two large American tugs which had been accompanying the convoy. The tugs tried to tow the *James Egan Lane* inshore far enough to beach her, but the torpedo damage was too great and the ship sank, on an even keel, in Whitsand Bay in about 12 fathoms of water, but with her bridge and superstructure showing above the waves. Captain Daymond on the *Boarhound* was instructed to pick the Captain of the sunken ship up at Millbay Docks and take him back to his ship. On leaving Millbay the crew of the *Boarhound* learned that an Admiralty tug had refused to take the job, as it was thought that there might still have been a U-boat in the vicinity. The American Captain then jovially filled the *Boarhound*'s crew with confidence by telling them that he had now been torpedoed twice, and wondered whether a U-boat would put 'a tin fish' into us, meaning the *Boarhound*, and make it a third for him. When the *Boarhound* arrived at the sunken ship, the American decided that he wasn't too keen to go back aboard so he was transferred to a mine watching drifter which was on station close to the wreck.

Close to Jupiter Point, on the River Lynher, near Saltash, lay three schooner hulks that had been abandoned on the foreshore, and filled with water every tide. The Admiralty decided that they had to be moved as they could become a possible obstruction with increased shipping on the run up to the D Day landings. Reynolds got the job of moving them. Firstly the shipwrights had to patch the hulks up enough to make them float again; then each was towed to Barnpool, in Plymouth Sound, and scuttled out of the way. Pumps would have been rigged, portables on board and probably one tug alongside with salvage suctions rigged into the hulk as well. There had to be no chance of the hulks sinking and causing an obstruction in the main fairway between Mount Edgcumbe and Devils Point.

In November 1945 the *Tactful* returned from Government service, the tug having spent most of the war on the Clyde, but she was not officially released from her charter until 11 January 1946. The *Briton* was also released on the same day, but it is thought that she never worked again being laid up in the Ballast Pond at Torpoint. The *Tactful* however was still a good tug, but required an extensive refit after her war service and on 25 March 1946 she was towed to Willoughby's Shipyard at Millbay for a complete refit. The fact that the refit was undertaken by Willoughby's and not in house at Torpoint, suggests that the reconditioning was paid for by the Ministry of War Transport.

During the war years, on 28 December 1943, the Torpoint and District General Supply Company Ltd became incorporated as a limited company. The shareholders and directors were Wilfred John Reynolds, a company director, of Coryton House, Torpoint; Arthur William George Reynolds, a general merchant of 2 Albert Terrace, Torpoint; Arthur Basil Reynolds, a company director of Udalgarth, Torpoint; and Walter Fearnley Reynolds a company director of Loch Lomond, Torpoint. Each held 100 £1 shares. Interestingly, W. J., A. B. and W. F. Reynolds were described as engineers when W. J. Reynolds Ltd was incorporated in 1926.

The foreman of the General Supply Co for many years was Walter Friend, who started off as a coalman driving a horse and cart delivering domestic coal all around the Rame Peninsula. Others working at Carew Wharf included Albert Tickle, Holly Tickle, Fred Webb, Albert White, Tom White, Terry Martin, and Colin Stacey.

The fleet moored on the trot off Torpoint in 1952. Right to left: ANTONY (2), TACTFUL, TREVOL, TRETHOSA, BAHIA, ALEXANDRA, BOARHOUND *and* WOLSDON. *Notice that the* TREVOL *has lost her wheelhouse and now has an open bridge.* W. J. REYNOLDS

CHAPTER SEVEN

THE POST WAR PERIOD

The end of the war in 1946 saw the various Reynolds' businesses in good heart. The busy war years had generated a healthy income. The tug fleet consisted of the *Antony* (2), *Trevol*, *Tactful*, *Alexandra*, *Bahia*, *Boarhound* and *Wolsdon*, with the *Briton* laid up at Carbeile Mill being dismantled.

In April the hopper *Claretta* was lifted by Admiralty salvage craft. It is not known when or where she sank but the barge was probably blocking a dock or passage and required moving quickly. On 7 May it was the turn of the *Alexandra* to be in trouble when she knocked 3 blades off her propeller whilst going alongside the battlecruiser *HMS Renown*. The *Alexandra* had a propeller which, unusually for the time, had each blade individually bolted on to the boss. It is more than likely that the tug was set down by the tide onto the *Renown*'s anchor cable whilst trying to manoeuvre a barge alongside the ship.

Another hopper (un-named) arrived in August from Great Yarmouth in tow of the wartime built tug *Empire Raymond*. The tug *Trevol* seemed to have emerged from the war with a different appearance. As built and in pre war years the *Trevol* was fitted with a wheelhouse on her bridge, but at some time during the war the wheelhouse was removed and all the post war pictures show the tug with an open bridge. Whether the wheelhouse was removed because it suffered damage during the war, possibly in an air raid, or whether it was just perhaps getting a bit rotten, is not known.

On 1 January 1947, all the staff, both ashore and afloat, began working a 44 hour week, reduced from a 48 hour basic week. On 23 July 1947, Reynolds Bros (Torpoint) Ltd. was incorporated, the first directors of the company being Fearnley, Arthur and Wilfred Reynolds. This limited company was set up to run the market gardening business which was carried on from the Mill Farm, where they also kept a large number of pigs. Why it should at this stage needed to be run as a separate enterprise is not clear, but it may have had something to do with tax liabilities or possibly farm subsidies, which may not have been available had the farm been run as part of the parent company. The Mill Farm was run by foreman Jack Dawe, along with Dan Glanville, George Cann, Frank Herd, Jack Heard and Mr Lang. As well as being a market garden, the horses were also stabled at the farm and the horsemen working in the Dockyard around this time included Harry Pearce, Fred Pearce, Charlie Leach, Dasher Rice, Jack Heale, Aeron Clements, Frank Cann, Mr Jenkins

Taken on board the TREVOL on a wet and windy day in 1949. Arthur Reynolds, wearing an army great coat and beret is standing on the left of the picture holding on to the mast stay. Arthur was a Major in the Royal Engineers during the Second World War and at this time was still commissioned in the Territorial Army. The American looking gentleman on the right is Frank Wiltshire, one of Reg Wiltshire's five brothers. Frank had come home for the first time, from Canada, where he emigrated in the 1930s, prospering and at one time becoming Mayor of Orilla. The identity of the well dressed lady in high heels, hardly appropriate wear for sailing on a tug, and the man seated next to her holding a file or sheaf of papers, remains infuriatingly obscure. It is just possible that they were film people making an early visit to view locations prior to the making of the film the CRUEL SEA in 1952.
DAVID MARTIN

and old Mr Holland. Gareth Hicks grew up in Torpoint and lived on the road used every day by the horses going to and from the Torpoint Ferry. If it was breezy, and both the front and back doors of the house were left open, the wind would blow the back door shut with a bang like a gunshot, and if the horses happened to be passing at the time, the shires would rear up on their hind legs; the horsemen were not amused. Gareth, like many Torpoint youngsters, remembers playing on the cut down remains of the tug *Cruden Bay* at Carbeile Creek. The middle section had been cut away to remove the engine and boiler, but the bow and stern were fairly intact.

Shortly after the war Reynolds' tugs were engaged in a less successful salvage. A foreign collier became stranded on the rocks at Jennycliff Bay. The *Boarhound* and *Antony* were soon on the scene and because of her shallower draft the *Boarhound* first made fast to the ship and tried unsuccessfully to pull the ship clear. The *Antony*, being deeper drafted could not get close to the ship so instead passed a rope to the bow of the *Boarhound* so that both tugs were pulling in tandem. The combined power however proved too much for the *Boarhound's* tow rope, which parted and before Reynolds' tugs could get re-connected, a large Dockyard tug , the

Atlas, arrived on tne rising tide, managed to get a line on board the casualty and pulled her clear – much to the consternation of the Reynolds' crews. Later, when the shelter of the Mount Batten breakwater was reached, thc *Boarhound* and *Antony* took over the tow and beached the ship in the Cattewater.

Joining the management at this time was Major Reginald Wiltshire, who had a distinguished military career in the Royal Engineers during the Second World War – it was said that he would have been recommended for a major decoration had not his commanding officer been killed in action. Reginald Wiltshire had trained as an architect before joining the army in 1937 and was married to Wilfred Reynolds' daughter Betty.

At the end of 1947 the boiler on the *Alexandra* (which was the original, installed when the vessel was built in 1902) failed. A replacement was sought and a second hand boiler in good condition was purchased in March 1948 from Friary Industries Ltd. The boiler came from a well known Plymouth vessel, the pilot cutter *Iridescence*, which had been replaced by a more modern cutter. The *Iridescence* was a wooden vessel 87 feet long and had been built at Macduff, Scotland in 1917, probably as one of many drifters built for the Government in the Great War. Given the Reynolds brothers many contacts it seems strange that they did not purchase the *Iridescence* themselves, especially if they needed a boiler. The boiler must have been in very good condition because many years later, in the 1960s, the safety valve jammed and the boiler pressure which was normally 180 PSI rapidly climbed to nearly 300 PSI before the frantic engineer managed to get the safety valve to lift (open) with a tremendous roar of escaping steam.

Plymouth as a port was booming. Commercial vessels would frequent Millbay Docks, Sutton Harbour, Cattedown Wharfs, and Victoria Wharfs. Imports were mainly coal and fuel oil at Cattedown; coal, fruit and grain at Millbay; and coal in Sutton Harbour. Ships at Oreston Quay and Pomphlett Lake, loaded outward cargoes of road stone. China clay and coke were also exported. In 1947 Sutton Harbour alone was handling over 200,000 tons of cargo a year, with Millbay Docks and the Cattedown wharfs recording significantly higher figures. Devonport Dockyard was also expanding again, creating ever more refuse (although by this time the majority of the naval ships were oil fired so there was not the volume of ash to be disposed of), and the ocean liner trade in Plymouth Sound had started again after the war with over 100 liners calling per annum.

Reynolds' other regular contracts included the Eddystone Lighthouse relief and a contract to tow a special barge carrying 100 ton concrete blocks from a block making plant at Oreston to Plymouth Breakwater. The tug fleet in 1948 was, to be charitable, getting on in years but in the main still in reasonable condition. The seven operational tugs had an average age of 46 years, the oldest the *Boarhound* being 68 years old and the youngest the *Trevol* 31 years.

Another large tug was needed, and after the war, as after the Great War, there were quite a number of wartime built Empire tugs of various classes on the market at fairly attractive prices compared to a new

The FIGHTING
COCK *on the River*
Mersey when owned
by the Liverpool
Screw Towage and
Lighterage
Company Ltd – the
'Cock Tugs'.
J. AND M.
CLARKSON / B
FEILDEN

building. One of the smaller ship handling Empire tugs would seem to have suited Plymouth admirably. So in 1949, to improve the fleet, W. J. Reynolds Ltd purchased another tug, but not a modern wartime built one, one slightly older, in fact only two years younger than the *Boarhound*!

The tug *Trethosa* was acquired from the Fowey Tug Company. This vessel was built in 1884 for the well known London tug owners William Watkins as the *Mona*. Because of long delivery dates in British shipyards at the time, the hull was built in Holland by Smit and Zoon of Kinderdijk. While the hull was being well built by a reputable tug building yard, for some reason Watkins gave the machinery order to the traction engine builders, Charles Burrell and Sons of Thetford, Norfolk, who built her large compound engine, developing 300 IHP, and the boiler. The boiler was 11 feet 6 inches in diameter and 10 feet long and weighed 25 tons. In order to transport the boiler to Kings Lynn Docks, for shipment to Holland, Burrell's had to construct a special low loading trailer which in itself weighed 14 tons, towed behind a large traction engine. The engine was, as far as can be ascertained, the second marine engine Burrells had built and was by far the biggest engine made at Burrells St Nicholas Works. As soon as the *Mona* was delivered to Watkins, she was sent to Le Havre to tow to Glasgow a disabled steamship, the *Niobe*. However, the tug did not complete the tow, as soon after setting out from Le Havre, the engine developed a fault which could not be easily repaired at sea. The *Mona* and her tow had to be towed into Cherbourg by French tugs, no doubt incurring a fairly substantial salvage claim. Such was the problem with the *Mona's* engine that another two Watkins' tugs were sent to France, one to tow the *Niobe* and one to tow the *Mona* back to London for repair, an ignominious start and one which must have cost Burrells dearly. What ever the nature of the problem, the engine was repaired and the tug deployed on more local jobs but it suffered further problems, and in less than a year Watkins decided they had bought a 'pup' and sold the tug at some considerable loss to the Cowes Steam Tug Co in 1885. She did not remain at Cowes for long and in 1890 was again sold, this time to the Queenstown Screw Tug Co at Cork, who ran the *Mona* for a further 12 years before selling the tug, in 1902, to the Liverpool Screw Towing and Lighterage Company, known to all as the 'Cock' tugs. On arrival at Liverpool the *Mona* was re-named *Fighting Cock* in keeping with the nomenclature of Cock tugs, but much more importantly, she was immediately sent to Laird Bros of Birkenhead (later Cammell Lairds) who completely rebuilt the engine, and from then on the tug became an extremely reliable unit. Apart from rebuilding the machinery, a cast brass cockerel was fitted to the mast, which the tug carried to the end of her days. In 1912 the Burrell boiler was removed and replaced with a new one, it is thought operating at a far higher boiler pressure, as the engine, which was when new rated at 300 IHP, after re-boilering was rated at 600 IHP (which could be accounted for by a substantial increase in boiler pressure).

Her Mersey career was long, and eventful. In 1906 the tug was in collision with the steamer *May*, and suffered bow damage. In 1923 the *Fighting Cock* rescued all the passengers and crew of the Isle of Man Steam Packet Company's steamer *Douglas* which sank in the Mersey after being run down in fog by the *SS Artemisia*; and in 1929 the tug herself was sunk after being run down by the sand dredger *G B Crow*. The *Fighting Cock* was quickly raised and refitted and returned to service.

After the Second World War, in 1947, the *Fighting Cock* was sold to Toyne Carter and Co, ships agents of Fowey, and renamed *Trethosa* and the same year the ownership was transferred to the newly formed Fowey Tug Co Ltd. Two years later in 1949, she was sold on to Reynolds. When the *Trethosa* arrived at Torpoint, all the lighting was by oil lamps, there was no electricity of any kind on board. Reynolds installed a petrol driven Stuart Turner generating plant in the engine room so that electric lights could be fitted. One engaging feature of the *Trethosa* was that during her time at Fowey and Torpoint her funnel had a noticeable list to port.

The towage rates for shipping in 1949 appear by today's standards ridiculously cheap, but they should be taken in context with the wage rates paid at the same period. For towing a ship from Plymouth Sound to any of the docks or wharfs at Millbay, Sutton Harbour or the Cattewater, the charge per tug was £5 for ships up to 250 net tons, £11 for ships up to 1,000 net tons and £17 for ships up to 2,000 net tons, larger vessels by negotiation. Often the larger ships would have three tugs, one forward,

The TRETHOSA ex-FIGHTING COCK ex-MONA at Torpoint. Note the cockerel at the masthead, a relic of her days as a Liverpool 'Cock' tug.
MARITIME
PHOTO LIBRARY

The TRETHOSA's *rare Burrell compound main engine. The steam reversing gear cylinder can be seen in the foreground, as can the underside of the wooden decks of the tug. The steam throttle valve control is the hand wheel on the bottom of the long spindle coming down from the main steam valve and the photograph is taken from where the engineer would stand to control the engine.*
GEORGE
WATKINS

one aft and one pushing up amidships. There was also an overtime surcharge for operating out of normal hours.

In 1951 the company began a pension scheme for the employees. It began on 1 December 1951. Engineer Eric Martin joined the scheme, and contributed 5 shillings a week out of his wages of about £7 per week.

In 1953 a film was made of the Nicholas Monsarrat book *The Cruel Sea* starring Jack Hawkins, and most of the location filming took place in Plymouth Sound. Although the opening sequences are supposed to be on the River Clyde, some of the dockyard shots were taken alongside the old London and South Western Railway wharf at Ocean Quay, Stonehouse, and others at various Devonport locations. In some early shots the *Trevol*

The equally rare steam steering engine on the TRETHOSA's bridge, which had a pair of oscillating cylinders driving the gear train through a hollow main spindle shaft. The steering could be either steam assisted when the tug was manoeuvring or docking ships, or hand only when making a longer journey. The large steering wheel was for hand steering and in front on the same shaft will be seen a very small wheel, used for steam steering. The compass on its binnacle can also be clearly observed. GEORGE WATKINS

can clearly be seen moored alongside the quay wall, and somewhat strangely the *Briton* appears alongside. The *Briton* by this time had been laid up out of use at Carbeile Mill (but was still externally intact) and it was most likely towed down to Stonehouse and hired out for some scenes later cut from the finished film. Most of the sea photography was taken by camera men on board the *Tactful*.

By 1954 both the *Bahia* and the *Boarhound* were starting to experience boiler problems, so were laid up at Carbeile Mill. Reynolds purchased another Fowey tug as a replacement. The *Gallant*, named after the sixteenth century Fowey Gallants who were privateers, had been built in Rye by the Rother Ironworks in 1884. Originally 77 feet long, in 1903 she was lengthened to 86 feet. The *Gallant* had a compound engine of 300 IHP. Until purchased by Reynolds, the *Gallant* had spent her entire career at Fowey, under various different owners but latterly the Fowey Harbour Commissioners. It was said she

TREVOL towing the Cunard cargo liner ANDRIA past Rusty Anchor in Plymouth Sound, The TRETHOSA is following astern. W. J. REYNOLDS

The GALLANT after lengthening in 1903, with a wheelhouse added to replace the open bridge.
AUTHOR'S COLLECTION

cost her owners nothing over the years, so much money did the tug make from numerous salvage jobs. She was regarded with great affection in Fowey, and kept in tip top condition. Also about this time, the *Trevol* suffered serious boiler problems and was partially dismantled at Carbeile Mill before scrapping.

As recounted in an earlier chapter, Reynolds had for many years a grid at the Ballast Pond at Torpoint for painting and below the waterline repairs. It was decided that something better was required. A second hand cradle slipway was purchased and Reynolds' men worked away installing the slipway at Carbeile Creek, near to the Mill. All the design work for the installation was undertaken by Reg Wiltshire (who it will be recalled had trained as an architect) and the concreting foundation work and steelwork was undertaken in-house. Amid great celebrations the first tug to use the slip was the *Alexandra*. This was a great improvement on the grid, as work could now be undertaken at all states of the tide, not just at low water. The cradle was hauled up by a large winch, and the winch was driven by the petrol paraffin engine and gearbox from an early Fordson tractor. Some dredging work had to be done at the seaward end of the slipway (by hand at low water) to accommodate the deeper drafted tugs;

The TREVOL being dismantled by Reynolds' own men at Carbeile Mill circa 1955.
W. J. REYNOLDS

and on occasions the slipway would be used to carry out repairs to other vessels, not belonging to Reynolds, thus providing useful extra revenue for the engineering works.

Over the years, it is thought that the largest ship slipped at Carbeile was the now famous schooner *Kathleen & May*, which for a number of years was preserved in Sutton Harbour. Reynolds' shipwrights fitted a new keelson, made out of old harbour piles, about 2 feet square, which had been removed from a wharf on the Cattewater in the early 1950s and saved by Reynolds. The outside

Opening of new slipway at Carbeile Creek, left to right, Captain Donald Hacker, master of the ALEXANDRA; Reg Southard, another long serving employee, joining Reynolds in 1919 and retiring in 1964; Major Reg Wiltshire, Fred Hannaford, Jack Dearden and Stan Toms.
MIKE DOHERTY

inch or so of the timber was badly eaten by gribble worm but the centre was sound, and the timbers were cut down on a big circular rack saw bench at the Mill. The bed of the saw was 36 feet long, and for a time driven by an old Messerschmitt engine. Later on another interesting vessel slipped and worked on was a large motor yacht the *Lanesra*, which belonged to Denis Hill Wood, at that time the Chairman of Arsenal Football Club - *Lanesra* is Arsenal spelt backwards. The original stone mill buildings at Carbeile had been supplemented by a couple of large Nissen huts, which housed much of the wood working and engineering machinery.

The first tug to be hauled up the new slipway, the ALEXANDRA. It is clear why the ALEXANDRA was a fast tug, her long lean lines can be observed. Cox of Co of Falmouth had the designing and building skills to build hulls that were 'just right'; fast with excellent sea keeping abilities and speed.
DAVID MARTIN

Looking from the winch house down the slip. In the background can be seen the WOLSDON towing a hopper barge away from Carbeile Mill. The stakes in the water are the moorings of the Admiralty timber ponds, where timber was kept afloat to stop it drying out too quickly whilst seasoning. DAVID MARTIN

The ALEXANDRA nearing the top of the slipway. Claude Reynolds is standing second right in the foreground.
DAVID MARTIN

The winch house and winding gear at the top of the new slipway.
DAVID MARTIN

W. J. Reynolds' only motor tug, the little VUSSEL in later guise with forward wheelhouse. This vessel was originally an Admiralty twelve oar rowing gig which was motorised and converted in house by Reynolds.
J. AND M. CLARKSON

Soon after the war, the floating workshop boat *Vussel* was suffering from severe rot in her keel, although the rest of the hull was in good order. The *Vussel* was hauled out of the water on a small slipway that Reynolds had constructed at Carbeile Mill (which pre dated the larger slipway built in the Creek), a new keel was fitted and the vessel was converted into a motor tender by Reynolds' own staff, fitting an engine and drilling the stern post to fit a stern tube and propeller. Decks were installed and a small wheelhouse built aft. The original steering was a tiller in the little wheelhouse. It was used as a general run around and work boat. When a job came up laying a cable across the River Tavy, the *Wolsdon* and *Vussel* were employed (this may possibly what the vessel was converted for in the first place). Much later, when in the 1960s Reynolds

won the contract to dump sewage effluent at sea, which will be described later, the wheelhouse on the *Vussel* was moved to a forward position, the steering changed to a wheel, a large towing post was installed and the launch was re-engined with a Kelvin 4 cylinder K series diesel; and then used to tow barges under Laira Bridge to Plympton sewerage works. The *Vussel* was used to lay a power cable across the River Yealm, crewed by Billy Hocking and Archie Ayres. The Reynolds family would use the *Vussel* as a pleasure boat. David Reynolds Martin, grandson of Claude Reynolds worked with the family firm in the school holidays in the 1960s and he recalled the *Vussel* being taken on fishing trips out into the Sound; and Jill Wiltshire, Reg Wiltshire's daughter also recalled using the *Vussel* for pleasure trips up the Tamar and stopping for picnics. At Trevol, adjacent to training base *HMS Raleigh*, just west of Carbeile Creek, the Navy used to have timber ponds, where new timber would be stored afloat in rafts to stop it drying out until needed. During a gale a large part of one of the rafts broke adrift, it was spotted by Reynolds' staff at Carbeile and the *Vussel* was quickly mobilised and saved the raft, possibly her only 'salvage' job.

Taken from the TACTFUL *a rare picture of one of the hoppers being towed at sea during dumping operations, showing the make up of the towing gear. A length of steel wire rope went from the tug's towing hook to just over the stern of the tug. The wire was used as it withstood the chafing on the tow rails and bulwarks better than rope. Connected to the wire is a length of about 120 fathoms (1 fathom equals 6 feet) of hemp or sisal towing hawser. This, when wet, gave the required elasticity to remove any shock loads caused by the tug and the barge rising and falling on the waves at different times. This in turn would be connected to either another short wire rope or heavy chain over the bow of the barge, again to take the chafe. Once wet, recovering this towing gear was a difficult job. If the weather was fine, a shorter tow rope would be used, which was easier to recover.* JILL WILTSHIRE

On board the CARBEILE, *engineer Michael Morgan (left) is standing on the engine room ladder looking out on deck whilst the stoker Micky Tresider is looking out of the galley/messroom.* MICHAEL MORGAN

CHAPTER EIGHT

CHANGING FORTUNES

The next period of the story covers the period from the mid 1950s and at the time of writing this narrative it is fortunate that there are still members of the Reynolds' family, as well as ex-employees who still have good memories of the business.

Michael Morgan was born in Torpoint in 1941 and at 15 years of age started an engineering apprenticeship with W. J. Reynolds Ltd at Carbeile Mill. Michael recalls that they could fix or make anything and he remembers an early job making large bolts, 1 inch diameter and 18 inches long, on a threading machine. They were used to repair the planking on some of the wooden hopper barges, whose planks could be 6 or 7 inches thick and the frames 10 inches.

During his apprenticeship Reynolds purchased another tug to replace the *Trevol*. This tug came from the Thames in 1957 as the *George Livesey* and had been built by the Lytham Shipbuilding Co in 1929 for the South Metropolitan Gas Company of London. The *George Livesey* was 82 feet long with a fine triple expansion engine of 550 IHP, in fact only the second engine of this type owned by Reynolds, the other being in the *Alexandra*. She was renamed *Carbeile* and later Michael Morgan was appointed as her engineer.

After this tug arrived Reynolds grew concerned, because although the tug was in excellent condition, Reynolds' crews could not get the boiler

The CARBEILE *when new as the* GEORGE LIVESEY *about to depart Preston Docks for London in 1929. A temporary wooden whaleback has been built to protect her foredeck during the delivery voyage and a lifeboat is carried over the towing rails on the after deck. Once on the Thames the tug would not be required to carry a lifeboat so no permanent provision was made for one.*
J. AND M. CLARKSON

The CARBEILE
dried out on
Torpoint foreshore
for bottom cleaning
and painting.
J. AND M.
CLARKSON

to steam properly – there was much head scratching. The problem was directly related to her previous owners, the Gas Board. In the manufacture of town gas, coal is heated in a retort to produce the gas and the residue material is known as coke, which will still burn, but has a far lower calorific value than coal. The furnaces on the *George Livesey* had been designed to burn coke and the firebars were too close together. Michael Morgan together with Reynolds' blacksmith, made up an experimental set of firebars, using steel flat bar normally used for making horseshoes. When these were fitted in the furnaces the problem was solved. This was not a permanent solution as mild steel firebars burn and bend very quickly so a new set of cast iron firebars was made at Willoughby's. The funnel was also lengthened to increase the draft.

On coming out of his apprenticeship Mike Morgan was doing general repairs on the fleet, and stints as relief engineer on the tugs. The *Alexandra* had an unusual propeller with bolt on blades. One day the

Alexandra was dried out on Torpoint foreshore with a blade missing. Michael was sent to fit the new blade. The remains of the old blade were removed and a spare blade from stock fitted. The next day found the *Alexandra* dried out once again on the foreshore – when the tug floated off after the repair, the vibration from the propeller was very bad. On measuring the blades it was found that the new one was over 1 inch bigger than the others which had worn over the years. Several hours were spent cutting and filing the new blade down to match the others and after that the propeller was nicely balanced and the vibrations disappeared.

After a time Mike Morgan was appointed as engineer on the *Carbeile*; the master was Dick Devereaux, mate Curly Palmer and stoker Rudge Carter. The *Carbeile* had steam reversing gear on the main engine and a steam turbine generator. The normal boiler pressure was 180 PSI. The tug had quite big coal bunkers and they would coal about once a month.

During this period the *Carbeile* was fully employed, moving hopper barges about in the Dockyard, assisting ships, timber and grain ships in and out of Millbay, large tankers to Cattedown Wharfs and stone boats at Pomphlett. One day, a shipping agent ordered a tug for Pomphlett and the *Carbeile* was sent to tow a stone boat out. The ships usually went head in to Pomphlett Lake and lay port side alongside the stone loading wharf. When loaded they were towed out stern first into the Cattewater and swung. It was blowing a severe gale and when the tug arrived the ship's captain did not want to sail. He went ashore to telephone his owners, and when he returned he told the *Carbeile* to make fast, his owners had apparently told him that if he was not prepared to go to sea, to pack his bags and they would send another master who would. This sort of situation was not unknown in coastal shipping in less regulated times.

On another occasion, the *Carbeile* was instructed to be head tug on a large Shell tanker heading for Cattedown Wharf. Some of these ships were 550 feet long with 28 feet draft and usually had three tugs. It was a poor day with a south westerly gale and on starting to turn to starboard to enter the Cobbler Channel (between the eastern end of the Hoe and Mount Batten) the tow rope parted and the tanker was heading straight for the rocks. The *Carbeile* was very handy and Dick Devereaux knew his job, he

The CARBEILE steaming past Torpoint. She was only the second Reynold's tug with a triple expansion engine. In Plymouth life saving was catered for by carrying a modern inflatable liferaft instead of a lifeboat.
MIKE DOHERTY

quickly spun the tug around, steamed in under the tanker's bow and picked up another line, and pulled the head of the ship to starboard into the channel, just in time.

In Plymouth it was usual for the tug to take a rope from the ship to tow on (in some ports the tug passes a special tow rope up to the ship). One ship passed down a brand new nylon rope, a material just starting to be used and a lot easier to handle than the old heavy manila ropes in common use. Once the ship was safely berthed, the *Carbeile*'s crew used the old tugman's trick and shouted to the crew on the focsle head of the ship to let go the tow rope, which they did and the tug crew quickly coiled it aboard the tug. On returning to Torpoint, Arthur Reynolds contacted the tug and said that the master of the ship had been on the telephone and wanted his rope back, so they had to return the rope to the ship.

Recalling some of the other tugs, Michael Morgan remembered the end of the *Gallant*. In the early 1960s this tug was going into the basin at Millbay Docks to tow a ship out. The engine was by this time getting very worn, and only had manual reversing gear. Because of the wear it had a habit if it wasn't caught at just the right moment, of becoming steam locked, steam both sides of the pistons, and wouldn't go ahead or astern. This happened and the tug hit the dock wall so hard that the boiler moved forward 2 inches. This was the end for the *Gallant*, which was then laid up and scrapped.

The *Trethosa* was held together with nuts and bolts (where rivets had worn away or fallen out) and big steel tie rods in the engine room. This tug did not do much work and was only steamed when the tug fleet was very busy or there was a pretty large ship to be handled. Usually Fernley Reynolds would sail as master. However, once the *Trethosa* got going she was very fast and could still pull well. One day after a job the *Trethosa* was returning to Torpoint to the trot where all the tugs were moored in a line. Fearnley conned the tug into position and skilfully picked up the mooring buoy. Once the mate had this secure on the foredeck, he rang down 'finished with engines' on the telegraph. Unfortunately, the telegraph chains were old and stretched so the needle on the repeater in the engine room only went round as far as 'full ahead', so the engineer obeyed the instruction and full ahead went the engine, the tug was charging about the trot until Fearnley, who had started to leave the bridge, ran back to the telegraph and rang 'stop.'

Captain Archie Ayers, who at the time of writing is still sailing as a master in sand dredgers, was brought up in Torpoint and lived near where the Yacht Club is today. As a small boy he had a little punt and was always helping the tugs when they came alongside the Ballast Pond at high water, and would often be given a trip on the tugs. When Archie was 15 Arthur Reynolds asked him if he would like a job on the tugs, Archie's mother had hoped to see him apprenticed to a trade in the Dockyard, but she knew he loved boats so allowed him to join Reynolds, even though this meant leaving school a little before the legal leaving age. His first job was as boy on the *Alexandra*, the Captain at this time was Donald Hacker. He didn't get off to a very good start. The *Alexandra* was dried out on the beach at Torpoint for bottom cleaning and the tide was out. The crew were all standing on the beach scrubbing the tug's bottom and Captain Hacker sent Archie climbing up a rope to get on board the tug, to make a pot of tea. Archie put the kettle on and then picked up the teapot and took it up on deck to throw the old cold tea over the side, which he did, but without looking below. The cold tea and tea leaves (no tea bags in those days) landed on the Captain, who was, to say the least, not best pleased. However, Captain Hacker took Archie under his wing and taught him a great deal.

On days when the tugs were quiet, the younger crew members had to help out on the Mill Farm or the engineering workshop. The farm was run by Jack Dawe who had suffered a brain haemorage at some time. On the farm was an old Fordson tractor, but Jack Dawe would have nothing to do

Captain Archie Ayers who started with Reynolds as a 15 year old deck boy and was latterly master of the tug CARBEILE *before transferring to Cory Ship Towage.*
ARCHIE AYERS

with it, he liked his horses, so Archie learned to drive it. At other times he was sent over to help in the Dockyard collecting the refuse and tipping it into the barges. By this time the horses and carts had been replaced by a fleet of elderly second hand lorries, a Dennis a Ford and an ex-US Army lorry amongst them, and Archie drove them all, even though he did not have a driving licence at the time.

In the Dockyard there were 79 stops or points were the lorries picked up the refuse and Reynolds' Dockyard foreman, who supervised all the collections and the loading of the barges, was Fred Lay.

Sometimes Archie would have to sail on the hoppers to assist with opening the doors and closing them. The hoppers had no rails around the outside of the deck (it wouldn't be allowed today) and no means of communicating with the tug except shouting and waving. One rough day Billy Hocking slipped and went over the side. Archie, who was noted for his prowess throwing a heaving line (a light rope ending in a special knot known as a monkey's fist, used for throwing to other vessels or ashore to pull the main mooring or towing lines with), quickly threw a line to Billy who managed to catch it, and the barge crew hauled him back aboard. He was lucky, even if the tug had stopped the barge would have carried on, and by the time the tug and barge could have turned around it would probably have been too late.

There was little demarcation in Reynolds, you had to go and do whatever job you were sent too. Archie was deckhand on the *Alexandra*, and coming in from one job the engineer, Archie Fursland, started to bank the boiler fires down a bit early, so that when the tug was moored at Torpoint he could get away home quickly. On nearing the mooring trot Arthur Reynolds shouted to them to go over to the Dockyard and pick up the loaded hopper *Claretta* and bring it back to the trot. Captain Donald Hacker, instead of picking up the moorings, rang down to the engineer for full ahead, but the engineer came up out of his engine room and said that there was no steam left (he having banked the fires too soon), and this resulted in the Captain and Engineer having a very heated argument on deck, with Archie Ayers having to try and steer the barely moving tug clear of the other river traffic.

On another occasion the *Alexandra* was towing in a hopper in and when approaching Mount Wise the sea tow rope was pulled in and the barge breasted up alongside. Shortly after an old rope tail which had been dumped in the hopper but had caught around the door chains and was dragging along under water, fouled the tug's propeller and brought the engine to an abrupt stop. They were fairly close to the shore and Archie had to strip off and swim for the shore to telephone for help. The tide was running strongly and to save him, if the tide swept him away, the master, Donald Hacker, tied a heaving line to Archie, which ended up with 3 heaving lines tied end to end and when the crew ran out of heaving lines they tied a mooring rope to the end, all of which made swimming very difficult. Archie managed to land ashore, find a telephone box and phone for help. The tug *Tactful* was sent down to tow the *Alexandra* and hopper back to Torpoint. Ropes in the refuse getting foul in the door chains were a constant problem. The barges were often beached on the grid at the Ballast Pond, and when dried out the chains would be slacked, allowing the doors to drop a couple of inches. The crews would then climb inside the hopper and cut off all the old ropes and wires.

Promotion came quickly, first to mate on the *Wolsdon* and then mate on the *Carbeile* with Dick Devereaux. Archie, keen to make an impression liked to keep the tug's paintwork in good order, but hard work would quickly discolour the buff paint on the funnel. If the tug had a day doing nothing, Archie would say to the Captain, 'Dick, shall I paint the funnel today?'. "Not today', replied Dick, 'it's too sunny and the paint will blister'. Another day, 'Dick, shall I paint the funnel today?' 'Not today, its too windy, the paint will splash on the wheelhouse' or 'Not today, the cows are going in so its bound to rain'; but eventually the funnel would get painted.

When Dick Devereaux retired, Jack Hocking became the master. And when Jack moved to the *Tactful* Archie became master of the *Carbeile*. Compared to the motor tugs which replaced the steamers when Cory's took over the business in 1973, the *Carbeile* was not very powerful, but Archie remembers her as being very handy. Her one fault was that she was very slow to raise steam in the mornings. Sometimes, especially after a weekend, if going down for a three tug job to Cattedown Wharf or Millbay, the *Carbeile* would be towed down by one of the other tugs to conserve steam and build up the boiler pressure. When pushing up on a tanker loaded with oil the fireman would still be stoking hard and if the wind was in the wrong direction, clouds of black smoke would be billowing across the tanker's deck, no spark arresters in the funnel either, so the pilot could sometimes not see the focsle head of the ship. This situation was confirmed by Captain Higham, a retired Plymouth pilot.

In the early 1960s Michael Morgan was relieving on the first *Tactful* and, when returning to Torpoint after a job, was up on deck when the fireman came up and shouted that there was water pouring out of the

The TACTFUL *on the slipway at Carbeile Creek.*
DAVID MARTIN

boiler. On entering the boiler room there was a stream of boiling water under pressure showering out from a hole just under one of the fireboxes. Michael quickly carved a piece of timber into a plug which he drove into the hole with a hammer, making a temporary repair. The tug was taken to Carbeile Mill, the boiler drained, and the firm's blacksmith spent three days welding inside the boiler patching up the thin areas. Mike Morgan said he was severely admonished by the boss, driving the plug in could have caused the boiler to explode, killing anybody down below.

Another mishap occurred to the *Carbeile* about this time. The tug with a barge was going alongside an aircraft carrier, *HMS Eagle*, on the inside, between the quay wall and the ship. The aircraft carriers were kept some distance off the quay walls by buffer pontoons. The master rang down for astern on the engine, but for some reason the relief engineer, not Michael Morgan, did not react quickly enough, the tug did not stop in time and one of the carrier's mooring wires knocked of the mast and funnel. The funnel was originally hinged, all Thames tugs were so fitted so that the funnels could be lowered for going under the many bridges, but at Torpoint it had been bolted together and stay wires rigged. The funnel was badly damaged and a new one had to be made and fitted.

A similar fate once befell the *Wolsdon*. Curly Palmer was the master, Rudge Carter the engineer and Archie Ayers the mate when they were towing a barge breasted up alongside (lashed alongside the tug instead of towing astern). There was a dredger anchored and working off the Dockyard. In the bright sunlight nobody noticed that the dredger had a wire rope stretching out to the quay wall to hold the dredger in position until, when nearly upon it, Archie saw the wire and shouted to Curly Palmer. Curly immediately rang the telegraph for full astern and Archie shouted down the engine room hatch to Rudge Carter but the *Wolsdon* did not stop in time and the wire sliced off the top of the wheelhouse and demolished the funnel. Archie ducked down by the side of the wheelhouse and when he looked up he saw Captain Palmer crouched on the deck of the wheelhouse below the wheel and then standing up to survey the damage from what had now become an open bridge. The *Wolsdon* was usually worked with just a three man crew with the engineer doing the stoking and the mate doubling as deckhand.

If there was an unexpected or rush job during the night, Arthur Reynolds would have to go round the houses of the crew members 'knocking them up'. Very few private houses had telephones but the firm could usually get a tug away in just over one hour, as the tugs would have the fires banked and the boiler would hold a fair amount of steam pressure overnight. Sometimes, on wild nights the crewman or his family did not hear the doorbell and Arthur had to resort to throwing stones at the bedroom window to attract attention (he must have known in which bedroom of each individual house his men slept).

When the Dockyard was refitting a warship, Reynolds would have to moor a barge alongside to remove the accumulated refuse. Often towards the end of the refit all surplus material had to be removed and all sorts of stuff ended up in the barge. This could include anything from brand new nuts and bolts, valves, good timber and a host of other things; some useful, some not. Because of the stores issue system in the Dockyard, once the material had been booked out to a job it could not be returned to the stores, even if it had not been used. Instead of the barge being towed straight out to dump, it would be towed to quay at Carbeile Mill and there a couple of labourers would sort through the barge and recover anything Reynolds could re-use, this kept Reynolds' engineering stores well stocked up. Michael Morgan rode a motorcycle and was involved in an accident in Plymouth, for which he was charged and fined. Fearnley Reynolds asked Michael how he was fixed to pay the fine (Michael was still an apprentice at this time), and on hearing that things were a bit tight Fearnley told Michael to go to the barge which had just come from a refitting ship, and get enough non-ferrous material – brass or bronze valves, etc – out of the refuse to sell to pay the fine.

On the normal refuse runs, the tug crews were adept at spotting anything that could be sold for scrap, and often on the way out to dump all sorts of stuff would be lifted out of the barge and stored aboard the tug. Coming up to Christmas this would be sold on to a local scrap merchant and the proceeds divided up between the crew. The recovered material would be transferred from the tug to the scrap merchant's boat and then one crew member would usually accompany the scrap man ashore to collect the cash. One year, the crewman had collected the cash and was walking back through Plymouth when Arthur Reynolds drove past and spotted him, it took some quick thinking to explain why he wasn't on board his tug where he should have been. No doubt Arthur knew exactly what was happening.

Launch of a new yacht at the small slipway at Carbeile Mill. The yacht was built by brothers Les and Reg Butson respectively shipwright and engineer at Reynolds. A redundant hopper barge lies at the Mill and the hull of the CRUDEN BAY *still lies on the foreshore in the distance.*
DAVID MARTIN

Captain Donald Hacker at the helm of the double ended clinker built rowing boat on an Eddystone relief job. Donald Hacker joined the merchant navy and sailed deep sea prior to joining Reynolds. He worked on the tugs for nearly 40 years but retired early in about 1965 after suffering a heart attack shortly before his 60th birthday. He died some 15 years later, just days before his great friend Captain Steve Hannaford also passed away. SHIRLEY ROWE

CHAPTER NINE

EDDYSTONE ROCKS
AND CONCRETE BLOCKS

For a very many years, in addition to the Dockyard refuse operations, Reynolds undertook two other major contracts, providing regular and valuable income. It would seem an appropriate time in the narrative to describe these jobs in detail.

The history of the various lighthouses built on the Eddystone Rocks, twelve miles outside Plymouth, has been very well told by several authors. Until comparatively recent times Eddystone, in common with all lighthouses, was manned 24 hours a day 365 days a year by keepers who normally worked a month on and a month off. The change-over of the Eddystone keepers was undertaken by Reynolds' tugs. Luckily, on occasions, members of the public were given the opportunity to join the tug crew on this work and have faithfully recorded the operation. In his book, *The Red Rocks of Eddystone,* author and journalist Fred Majdalany, who incidentally was educated at King William's College on the Isle of Man (as was your author), was able to sail on such a relief. Fred recalls boarding the tug at 10.30 in the morning at Millbay Docks, and sailing to the Eddystone. Once out past the calm waters inside the Breakwater, the tug began to pitch and roll, slopping water over the bows. It took

The ALEXANDRA getting ready to sail for the Eddystone with a Trinity House keeper in uniform on board.
DAVID MARTIN

The Eddystone Lighthouse, nearly 13 miles from Plymouth, Reynolds' men and a keeper being transferred can be seen in the bottom left of picture.
AUTHOR'S COLLECTION

about an hour and a half to reach the lighthouse. The tug would be towing a double ended ship's lifeboat, to which extra strong mooring posts had been fitted. On the way out the keeper joked with the tug crew about the possibility of the transfer being aborted due to the weather; in fact in the winter, it was rare for a transfer to take place on the allotted day. Once the tug reached about a quarter of a mile from the rocks she was stopped and four of the five man tug crew and the keeper transferred to the small boat, leaving only one man on the tug. The boat was then rowed towards a gulley in the rock by the four members of the tug crew. On nearing the gully, and when in the correct line of approach, which meant lining up the lighthouse door and the steps below, an anchor was dropped over the stern of the boat and the anchor scope (rope) was allowed to pay out. The tug master, who was in charge, and who was one of the two forward oarsmen, together with the other forward oarsman, stood up and used the oars to fend off the rocks and steer the boat in. When actually in the gulley, the men at the lighthouse threw down heaving lines to which mooring ropes were attached, and these were hauled on board the boat and

Reynolds' men transferring a keeper from lighthouse. The crew in boat are thought to be George Prescott, Steve Hannaford, Donald Hacker and Stan Bradford, all very experienced in the transfer. If work for the other tugs was slack, often the masters would go out on the relief, the men also received an extra 'danger money' payment for the job, in the 1950s it was 2/6d per man.
W. J. REYNOLDS

made fast, as was the anchor scope aft. The boat was now held, rising up and down on the swell, by two lines forward attached to the lighthouse and the anchor laid out aft.

Once the boat was secure, another rope was thrown down from the lighthouse, this one attached to a hand winch inside the building. The tug master tied a bowline part of the way up and a good length was coiled in the boat. The lighthouse keeper then used the bowline as a foot hold and hung onto the rope, which the keepers inside the lighthouse started to haul up. The tug master controlled the angle of the rope by deftly paying it out from the boat, until the keeper was landed on the narrow ledge or stand off built into the base of the lighthouse. Stores were sent up by the same method and the keeper coming off returned the same way, being heaved towards the boat by the tug crew. The only concession to safety was that the men being transferred wore a heavy old fashioned life jacket. The method in the 1950s hadn't changed for years.

In 1933, Martin Langley, a well known maritime author and expert on west country shipping matters, made a trip out to the Eddystone in the tug *Boarhound* with Captain William Daymond. Martin recalled that Captain Daymond's son Stan, at that time a crewman with his father, who later also became a master with Reynolds, told of many trips which had to be aborted due to bad weather.

Ralf Farrell was stoker then engineer on the *Alexandra* under Captain Donald Hacker. He recalled that coming up to Christmas one year, the tug had made several abortive attempts at making the transfer, each failing because of bad weather. However, even though conditions were far from ideal, the relief was finally achieved on Christmas Eve, and the keepers coming off gave each crew member of the tug a £5 tip, so pleased were they to get off before Christmas. No doubt the keepers going on duty might have wished the weather to remain boisterous for a little longer.

Reynolds' men returning to the tug ALEXANDRA *at the Eddystone. The crew are, sitting down rowing in bow George Prescott, mate and later master of the* ALEXANDRA; *standing starboard side Stan Bradford; standing port side Buss Williams and steering aft Donald Hacker.*
SHIRLEY ROWE

The special Camel barge used to carry the 100 ton blocks out to the seaward side of Plymouth Breakwater. In this stern view the gap in the centre of the barge, which fitted exactly around the 100 ton blocks, is clearly visible, as are the two large suspension girders from which the block hangs during transit.
MIKE DOHERTY

Ralf Farrell originally started at 15 years old with Reynolds as an apprentice to the blacksmith, Alfie Cook, at Carbeile Mill. After about 9 months the blacksmith's son left school and he too was taken on as an apprentice blacksmith, and it was obvious to Ralf that the father, quite naturally, wanted his son to take over. Because of this Reynolds moved Ralf to become a stoker on the tugs, mostly on the *Alexandra* but also on the *Carbeile* and at different times on all the tugs. Eventually the firm stopped using the *Alexandra* for the Eddystone relief as, although she was fast, her bottom plating was getting thin, and in her later years had much concrete poured into the bottom to keep her water tight. The worry was that in heavy weather, the banging about might crack the concrete which could result in the tug sinking. (It has always been a common practice to make temporary repairs to vessels by putting in what is known as a cement box, which in effect means concreting over an area of thin or leaking plates.) After 12 years on the tugs, Ralf Farrell left to take up civilian employment at *HMS Raleigh* at Torpoint. Russell Tinns took over as stoker, remaining with the firm and then moving like many Reynolds' men to Cory's tugs when the firm was taken over in 1972.

Side view of the Camel barge at the Breakwater Quay, Oreston.
MIKE DOHERTY

Plymouth Breakwater, nearly a mile long was built between 1813 and 1833, and was a masterpiece of civil engineering in its day. It was designed to give protection to the Cattewater and the Hamoaze, a function which it still admirably fulfils, and like the Eddystone Lighthouse, has been well documented over the years by a number of authors. One of the problems encountered with the Breakwater has been the erosion of the outer armour material and fill by wave action on the seaward side, and this has always been

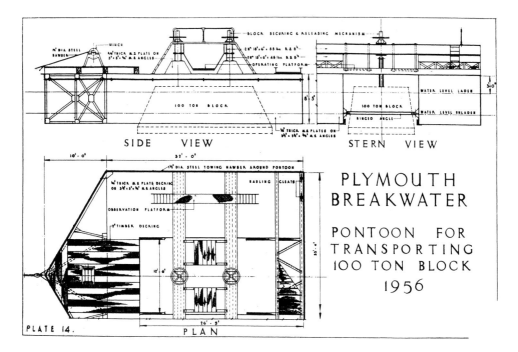

*General
arrangement plan
of the Camel barge.*
MIKE DOHERTY

repaired and reduced by dumping initially large stones and then later on, in the twentieth century, by large concrete blocks.

Experiments with blocks of various shapes and sizes eventually proved that blocks of an elongated pyramidal shape weighing 100 tons, provided the best form for breaking the seas and reducing erosion to the Breakwater. During the experiments the blocks, some of which weighed over 200 tons, were cast on site at low water. But this was fraught with difficulties, the shuttering being washed away or damaged by wave action. The engineers then tried using steel moulds, redundant pontoons, towed out and sunk and then filled with concrete. Eventually two of the pontoons were joined together and adapted for carrying 60 ton blocks from the shore.

In order to facilitate the initial construction of the Breakwater a quay was built at Oreston on the Cattewater and the millions of tons of stone used in the construction was obtained from quarries adjacent to the quay. The quay remained the base for loading materials for maintenance and became the site for casting the blocks, once a method of moving them out to site had been developed.

In 1928 Philip and Sons of Dartmouth built a special pontoon to carry the blocks, each weighing 100 tons. The pontoon was shaped like an angular letter U laid down flat. It had a bow section and two sides with a rectangular gap in the middle. The gap was straddled by two massive girders and on each girder was a release mechanism and operating platform. The pontoon was 42 feet long with a beam of 33 feet, empty it had a draft of just less than 2 feet which increased to 5 feet 3 inches when loaded.

The 100 ton blocks as cast in the river bed of the Cattewater. At high water the Camel barge would be floated in around the block and when the tide went out the barge would be sitting on the bottom around the block. The suspension quick release mechanism would then be connected and on the next high tide the barge would lift the block off the bottom and Reynolds would tow it to site. The blocks were cast on a concrete base in the river bed; each base was exactly the right distance apart to allow the Camel barge to be placed around any block.

MIKE DOHERTY

The blocks were cast in moulds set on bases in the bed of the river, which dries out at low water. Once the concrete had set, the moulds were removed and the block was ready for up lifting. The pontoon, which was known as the 'Camel' was floated in so that the open stern part floated around the block at just the right time on a falling tide. At low water the Camel pontoon would be sitting on the bottom with the block in the middle. The block had two lifting points cast in, and the release mechanism on the barge was connected to the block and tightened up. As the tide came in, and the depth of water increased, the pontoon lifted the block off the bottom. It was then ready for towing to site – the Camel pontoon with the block hanging down below.

The pontoon and block were then towed very slowly out to the seaward side of the Breakwater, sometimes taking up to one and a half hours to cover the three mile distance, as the tug would be fighting the incoming tide. Usually four men would man the pontoon to handle the mooring lines and operate the release mechanism. On arrival a small motor boat would run lines from the Camel pontoon to the Breakwater and the tug would drop her anchor to seaward, and so hold the Camel in position, the exact spot being determined by engineers on the Breakwater. Once in position the release mechanism would be activated and the block would drop a few feet to the bottom. It was arranged to try and drop the block when there was not much water underneath so it did not drop too far, which may have broken the block. When released from its 100 ton load the Camel shot up out of the water, the crew on board having to hang on. The shore lines were released and the tug towed the Camel back to Oreston. From 1928 until fairly recently, apart from the war years, an average of 50 blocks a year were placed.

In 1956 the original Camel of 1928 was replaced with a new one of the same design, and at this time Reynolds were charging £27.10.0d to tow out each block, with a £2.10.0d surcharge on Saturdays and Sundays.

The *Alexandra* was often used for the block placing, her draft was lighter than the bigger tugs which made the positioning on site a bit easier, but most of the tugs undertook the job at some time.

Like the Eddystone relief, block placing was very weather dependent and it was not unknown to set off from Oreston Quay with the pontoon in tow, only to find that by the time the Breakwater was reached about an hour and a half later, the wind had freshened or the swell built up too much and the releasing of the block had to be postponed. The barge with the block still hanging below then had to be towed back, which often took longer as by this time the tide would usually be ebbing and the tug would be pulling the awkward tow against the tide and the flow of the River Plym coming out of the Cattewater.

The block placing did not always go to plan. On one occasion the Camel pontoon with block hanging below was towed out by the *Alexandra* and when arriving seaward of the Breakwater the wind had freshened, blowing the tug towards the Breakwater. Because of the rising swell the motor launch running the lines from the pontoon to the Breakwater was having difficulty and the *Alexandra* was blown too far inshore and in trying to turn, her propeller hit one of the submerged blocks and knocked some of the blades off. The *Alexandra* was in a dangerous situation and the normally imperturbable Donald Hacker was said to be somewhat agitated. The situation was saved by the motor launch towing the *Alexandra* far enough to seaward to allow the anchor to be let go, and wait for another of the tugs to come out and tow her back to Torpoint for repair.

Captain Donald Hacker pictured on board a tug thought to be the GALLANT. Note the forward towing hooks fitted in front of the wheelhouse. Were these fitted by Reynolds and if so, why? The reason for them now remains obscure. The tug may have been used as a stern tug on a long tow, or they may have been simply to provide a strong quick release mechanism for placing mooring blocks and chains slung over the bow of the tug. If used for the former, the mast would have had to be removed as it was situated ahead of the position of the hooks.
SHIRLEY ROWE

The ANTONY (3) and a British India C class ship in the entrance of Millbay Docks. MIKE DOHERTY

CHAPTER TEN

BIG SHIPS
AND BOVRIL BOATS

By 1960 Plymouth was importing over 1,120,000 tons of cargo with a healthy export trade in china clay and stone. The biggest growth had been in the import of petroleum spirits, increasing from about 80,000 tons after the end of the war to just under a million tons in the 1960s. The tankers were becoming ever larger, stretching the limited room in the Cattewater. Tankers such as Dutch Shell's *Korovina*, a steam turbine powered tanker of 12,121GRT. This class of ship was just over 555 feet long with a beam of just less than 70 feet and had a summer draft of 29 feet 10 inches, loading about 18,000 tons of cargo. These ships needed three tugs and were assisted up to a swinging ground off Turnchapel where they would be turned and towed stern first up to Cattedown wharf. Normally there would be one tug ahead and one astern with the third pushing the ship alongside.

In 1959 Reynolds had available three reasonably powerful tugs, the *Trethosa* at 600 IHP, the *Antony* at 585 IHP, and the *Carbeile* at 550 IHP. However the *Trethosa* was little used and the 400 IHP *Tactful* was often the third tug. In other ports usually frequented by these tankers the tugs would more normally be in the 800 to 1000 horse power class at this time. This no doubt prompted Reynolds to seek some more powerful vessels and in 1960 they found for sale at Bristol the R. and J. H. Rea tug *Corgarth* which had been built at Falmouth, as one of two sisters, by Cox and Co in 1921. The *Corgarth* was 90 feet long with triple expansion engines of 650 IHP. On arrival on the River Tamar the tug was renamed

The ANTONY (3) ex-CORGARTH, acquired in 1960, towing in Fowey.
PAUL RICHARDS

*ANTONY (2) ex-
COMMONWEALTH
being dismantled by
Reynolds' own men
at Carbeile slipway
in 1960.*
PAUL RICHARDS

Still able to show a good turn of speed at nearly 80 years old. the TRETHOSA steaming past Plymouth Hoe on her way back to Torpoint, not long before she was scrapped.
MIKE DOHERTY

1960 at Torpoint. Left to right: ALEXANDRA, CARBEILE, ANTONY (3) one of the hopper barges, and TRETHOSA (note the latter's funnel which always had a list to port)
DAVE HOCQUARD

The TRETHOSA *at the breaker's yard, on Marrowbone Slip, Sutton Harbour 1964.*
PAUL RICHARDS

The TREVOL (2) *ex-*RAEGARTH, *built by Cox and Co Falmouth in 1921.*
DAVID MARTIN

to become the third *Antony*. The second *Antony* of 1902 was scrapped at Carbeile Mill. Two years later, the sister ship the *Reagarth* came on the market and Reynolds bought this vessel, which had also spent her entire career with Rea's at Bristol, and renamed the tug to become the second *Trevol*. This marked the end for the old *Trethosa*. She was sold for scrapping at the Barbican in Sutton Harbour in 1963, just one year short of being 80 years old; not bad when considering that when the tug was delivered new, it was regarded by her first owners as an abject failure. How many tugs built today will have such a working life?

Whilst the ship towage side of the business was booming, a black cloud was appearing over the horizon which would threaten and ultimately end one of Reynolds' oldest contracts. Public opinion, voiced by the conservation lobby, was concerned about the damage to the marine environment caused by dumping refuse at sea, and the inhabitants of the coasts around Whitsand Bay (the dumping ground) were constantly complaining about refuse being washed ashore on the beaches. From the 1960s there have been successive pieces of legislation which have gradually outlawed the practice of sea dumping except for dredged material, and under strictly licensed terms. This did not happen overnight but in the early 1960s there were definite 'rumblings'. Captain Archie Ayers recalls that around this time Reynolds were operating the hopper barges *Clearwell*, *Claretta*, *Fowey* (probably *FHC No 2*), *Pompey* and *Brook*,

the latter being a slightly smaller hopper barge, and a coal barge the *Test*. The *Clearwell* and *Claretta* were big barges and could normally hold two days refuse but the others were usually filled in a day.

The *Test* would be filled up with coal at Carew Wharf and taken out to each tug so that bunkering could be carried out, at any state of the tide, on the trot. In earlier times the tugs would have to come alongside Carew Wharf or the Ballast Pond to coal at high water. The *Test* had a mast and derrick, and a motor winch driven by a Lister engine to lift the baskets of coal up to the bunkers of the tugs. All hands had to coal, and Archie Ayres said that after coaling, you were black, the coal dust got everywhere; the deck hands and boys would be in the barge shovelling the coal into baskets. The *Test* would be towed out by the *Vussel*.

Another small craft owned by Reynolds was an ex-RAF launch, called the *Maud*, which had the engine removed. This was equipped as a floating workshop with the welding plant and oxy acetelene burning gear that had originally been installed in the *Vussel* and removed when that launch had been motorised.

There was still usually at least one barge a day to be towed to sea to dump but when the 'Fleet' was in, extra barges would be required. On occasions, when the weather was very bad, the loaded barges would be moored off Torpoint and it could get to the stage when all the barges were full and none would be available to fulfil contractual obligations the next day. Certain trusted employees, would, on such occasions, row out to the moorings at the dead of night, when the tide was ebbing and a strong current was running out of the Tamar, and often in heavy rain, to check that the moorings were in order. Occasionally, in the dark, somehow the chains on the hoppers would be accidentally released and the contents emptied into the river. The sound of the wind and rain would usually muffle the sound of the rattling door chains on the hopper barge, so that it could not be heard from ashore, and the ebb tide and current of the river

CARBEILE (left) and ANTONY towing a British India C class ship (about 465 feet long) away from Millbay Docks. MIKE DOHERTY

*WOLSDON (ahead)
and ALEXANDRA
(alongside) towing
a Torpoint floating
bridge to the
scrapyard in Sutton
Harbour, March
1961*
DAVE
HOCQUARD

would carry the cargo out to sea in the dark. The fortuitous result, a couple of empty barges ready for the Dockyard the next morning!

To digress slightly, the Mill Farm would, coming up to Christmas, fatten upwards of 100 turkeys and geese, and in the weeks prior the Christmas the firm's shipwrights would make special wooden packing cases which would traditionally be used to send plucked and dressed birds, as a thank you, to various high ranking officials in the Dockyard and at the Admiralty in London, local shipping agents, and ship owners. Many of the wives of employees would be called in to help pluck and dress the poultry. Another Christmas tradition was a Christmas day football match, played of course on the pitch established on the site of the Carbeile Mill pond, between a team of the land based employees of the company, known as the Mill Hotspurs and a team from the tug and barge crews, known as the Mariners.

Another trade in decline was the weekly Friday evening ritual of supplying coal to bunker the Torpoint ferries. In 1960 two new diesel electric ferries came into service and by 1966 the last steam ferry was scrapped when a third diesel electric ferry arrived.

Captain Jack Hocking joined Reynolds in 1958 and quickly moved up the promotional ladder. His father had also served many years in Reynolds' tugs. In his time Jack was master of the *Alexandra*, which he recalls as being very hard to steer with a huge wheel. The second *Tactful*, had an open bridge and was very uncomfortable in the winter. Jack also recalled that the *Carbeile*, when she first came down from London, was not allowed to go outside the Breakwater. The tug had fairly low bulwarks in common with most Thames tugs designed primarily for barge towing. When Jack became her master, he found that because of this restriction (placed on the tug by Reynolds themselves) he and his crew were missing out on overtime, and he persuaded Arthur Reynolds that the tug was

more than capable. After that the *Carbeile* took her turn towing the hoppers out and the crew got their overtime.

Sometimes, if the weather had been bad there might be two or three hoppers to dump, two or three tugs would each take one hopper barge, but if the other tugs were busy elsewhere, one tug would have to dump all three. Each round trip out to the dumping ground took three or four hours, sometimes more if the refuse was buoyant and would not drop out, and it could be midnight when the tug finally returned to pick the mooring up at Torpoint.

When Brittany Ferries started a service from Roscoff to Millbay Docks, Captain Hocking docked the very first ferry with the *Carbeile*. During the '60s there were large Russian trawlers, Fyffes banana boats and grain boats all going to Millbay. Captain Hocking said that sometimes in bad weather, when docking ships at Millbay, the tug could get stuck in a corner as there was hardly any room to manoeuvre, and one of the other tugs would have to pull the first tug clear.

Taken from the foredeck of the CARBEILE *as the tug assists the* ST MERRIEL *at Millbay.* ANTONY *on the stern of the ship.*
MIKE DOHERTY

The ANTONY *(ahead) and* CARBEILE *towing an RFA tanker* BLACK RANGER *towards the Hamoaze.*
MIKE DOHERTY

The ALEXANDRA about to tow the Everards ship SIMILARITY (built 1951 1575grt) away from Pomphlett stone wharf. Mike Doherty was fortunate in the 1960s to be given many opportunities to sail on the tugs and on one occasion he was aboard the ALEXANDRA which sailed to Pomphlett to tow out an Everards ship. It was snowing, a near blizzard, and when the ALEXANDRA reached Pomphlett the ship had not completed battening down the hatches, so the tug moored alongside the ship until it was ready to sail. The Everard ship's chief engineer, came up from his engine room and looked down at the ALEXANDRA, and could hardly believe what he saw, a floating 'relic from the past'. He jumped aboard the tug and went below and was enthralled at the wonderful condition of the Cox built triple expansion engine.
RICHARD COX COLLECTION

    Reynolds' tugs also handled a lot of the Royal Fleet Auxiliary ships going up to Devonport. One interesting job Jack Hocking undertook in the *Carbeile* was transporting a 50 ton propeller from Devonport to Falmouth Docks, it was a spare for a ship refitting at Falmouth. A special frame was built on one of the hopper barges and the propeller lifted on and lashed down, and safely delivered to Falmouth Docks. Major Reg Wiltshire, who was at this time running the firm together with Arthur Reynolds, had arranged the job and he travelled down to Falmouth by road to see the propeller safely unloaded.

    Jack lost the end of a finger when the tug was assisting a cable ship to moor at a buoy in the Cattewater. The tug was passing the ship's line to the buoy and the crew were struggling to try and get the pin in the shackle, Jack jumped across to assist but the ship surged a bit, tightening the mooring chain, and trapping the end of his finger in one of the links and taking it off. One of the crew, engineer David Callow, found the end of the finger and thinking that a hospital might be able to sew it back on, quickly threw it onto the deck of the tug. Unfortunately the finger never reached to tug, when in mid air, a hungry seagull swooped down, caught the finger and ate it!

Alan Wade was a young man from Launceston, a mason by trade, who with some friends came to Plymouth looking for work, and a good time. He was taken on by Arthur Reynolds, bricking up the furnaces, and then became a stoker serving on all the tugs as different times, and marrying Jack Hocking's sister. 'Reynolds were wonderful bosses', Alan recalled, 'and Reg Wiltshire, an ex-army man was a real gentleman'.

Reynolds certainly looked after their employees. It was not uncommon, if a staff member was setting up home or buying a house, for Reynolds (usually one of the family in a private capacity) to provide a loan for the deposit or furniture, paid back over time out of the man's wages. As well as engendering loyalty from the employees (although working for Reynolds was a good, well paid job with plenty of opportunity for overtime, and consequently many staff spent their entire working lives in Reynolds' employment) it showed shrewd business acumen, as the key employees were to a certain extent beholden to their employer.

As well as working in Plymouth, Reynolds' tugs would assist large vessels at Dartmouth and Fowey. The Fowey Tug Co and later the

Cable ship JOHN W MACKAY arriving at Plymouth and approaching the Cobbler Channel with the ANTONY (3) and TREVOL (2) in attendance.
DAVE HOCQUARD

The aged GALLANT raising steam at Torpoint, with the wooden rowing boat for crew access alongside.
MARITIME PHOTO LIBRARY

The GALLANT being scrapped in Sutton Harbour c.1964. PAUL RICHARDS

The TACTFUL *being dismantled at Marrowbone Slip in Sutton Harbour about 1964.*
PAUL RICHARDS

Harbour Commissioners operated their own tugs, but if one was off service for overhaul or repair, Reynolds often sent a tug to Fowey to assist.

By 1964 the *Tactful* had reached the end. Her boiler sufferd problems in the early 1960s, and it was its contnuing deterioration that finally finished her. As a replacement Reynolds were fortunate, in 1965, to purchase another tug from Fowey. The *Tolbenny* had been built by Fellows and Co of Great Yarmouth in 1928 for the well known London ship owners F. T. Everard & Sons, and launched bearing the company name as the *F T Everard*. The tug went to Fowey in 1951, renamed *Tolbenny*, under the ownership of the Fowey Tug Co, and was taken into the ownership of Fowey Harbour Commissioners in 1961, when they took over the towage services in the port. The *Tolbenny* was 83 feet long with a triple expansion engine developing 550 IHP, and had forced draught fans in her boiler room. Originally the tug had been of the fairly standard Thames lighterage tug design, but at Fowey her bridge was rebuilt and a lifeboat

As built the TACTFUL *(2) on trials as the F T* EVERARD. *Judging by the smoke coming from the funnel and the steam from the safety valve, and the obvious turn of speed, and the lifeboat being carried aft of the hook, this photograph was probably taken on the trials when brand new.*
RONALD STANFORD

The TOLBENNY of Fowey Harbour Commissioners. Notice the rebuilt bridge and lifeboat fitted at Brazen Island Shipyard, Fowey.
AUTHOR'S COLLECTION

added to make her suitable for sea towing. Reynolds paid £1,750 for the tug, which was a good buy, but the price reflected the fact that by this time steam tugs were regarded as a thing of the past, most tug owners going over to diesel powered vessels. To make a comparison, Gaselee and Sons Ltd, who were also an old family towage business, based on the Thames, built a new motor tug, the *Culex*, of roughly the same dimensions and power as the *Tolbenny*, delivered in 1958. It cost Gaselee's £59,720. Reynolds renamed the *Tolbenny* to become the second *Tactful*. At Fowey the tug had an open bridge, and Reynolds built a sort of a forward facing wheel shelter, not a full wheelhouse, which gave the master some limited protection from the weather in the winter months. Unfortunately, this did nothing to improve the looks of the tug and with the skilled craftsmen at Reynolds' disposal it is difficult to understand why a full wheelhouse was not built.

The TACTFUL (2), in W. J. Reynolds ownership, leaving Fowey after assisting a ship. Notice the small wheel shelter fitted ahead of the open bridge.
PAUL RICHARDS

CARBEILE on the slipway at Carbeile Creek, for overhaul. March 1966.
PAUL RICHARDS

In September 1964 the *Western Morning News* newspaper carried an article about the tugs, and Fearnley Reynolds, W. J. Reynolds' only surviving son at that time, said that the firm charged about £150 per ship to tow a 10,000 ton ship into the port, usually three tugs inwards, with a similar charge for the outwards movements, but normally with only two tugs. Fearnley lamented on the decreasing workload stating 'It is surprising how slack the work is, present day business is not like the old days. We could do with a lot more.'

At the time of the arrival of the *Tactful* from Fowey the tugs were manned in the main by men who had seen long service with Reynolds.

Three Reynolds masters sitting on one of the crew boats at the Ballast Pond, Torpoint. Left to right: Dick Devereaux, Ron 'Curly' Palmer and Jack Hocking.
JACK HOCKING

The master of the *Trevol* was Stan Bradford with Tony Spiller as mate and Reg 'Spot On' Butson as engineer; The *Antony* had Steve Hannaford as master, with Jack Hocking as mate and Eric Martin as engineer; *Carbeile*, master Dick Devereaux, mate Archie Ayers, engineer Michael Morgan; *Tactful*, master Ron 'Curly' Palmer, mate Charlie Armstrong, engineer Rudge Carter; *Alexandra*, master George Prescott, Donald Hacker having retired, mate Danny Medway and engineer Archie Fursland; *Wolsdon* had as her master a Captain Clayton, who was the only man since the 1920s to join the firm as a master, and the only one ever to hold a masters certificate. (Until 1980 when the rules were changed, no certificate was needed to command a ship in the Home Trades provided the vessel did not carry more than 12 passengers, so the vast majority of tugs, dredgers and coasters were manned by uncertified, but none the less very competent, masters and mates.) In Reynolds however, most of the engineers had served an apprenticeship with the firm before being promoted.

Name	*M. Morgan*					
Week ending	10 . 12 . 60					
WAGE		7	5	7		
OVERTIME			7	9		
INCOME TAX REFUND					7 /3	4
INCOME TAX			9	0		
NATIONAL HEALTH INS.			9	11		
SUPERANNUATION						
					/8	11
				TOTAL	6 /4	5

2956

W. J. REYNOLDS, Ltd., TORPOINT

W. J. Reynolds Ltd. wages slip for engineer Michael Morgan, 10 December 1960.
MICHAEL MORGAN

Murray Hyslop's father was Eric Martin, engineer on the *Antony* and he recalled that as a boy, if a ship was being docked or taken to sea at the weekend, he would often accompany his father. Some two hours before the tug was due to leave the moorings at Torpoint, the engineer and stoker would scull out from the Torpoint Ferry beach in a big clinker built rowing boat. Each tug had its own boat (otherwise if the first crew took their boat out to the tug the other crews would have no means of getting aboard). Once aboard the stoker would clean the banked fires and add fresh coal whilst Eric would check around and oil up the big triple expansion engine. For much of this time the stoker was Ronnie Wilson who in his spare time was the local Scout Leader. Once the engine was oiled up and the steam pressure in the boiler had increased, the engine would be turned over slowly a few revolutions ahead and astern and the stoker would then scull back ashore and pick up the rest of the crew. Once aboard, the mooring would be slipped and the tug would set off down to the Cattewater or Millbay. During the trip down, the master Steve Hannaford who walked with a slight limp, would allow the young Murray in the wheelhouse, but once the rope had been connected to the ship and the tug started pulling he had to go below decks to the engine room (to avoid getting caught by the tow rope) where he would watch his father operating the engine controls in response to the orders on the telegraph.

When the *Antony* needed scrubbing under water, the tug was put on the beach at Torpoint and usually the opportunity was taken to clean the boiler as well. Once the outside work had been carried out at low water over a couple of tides, either the *Alexandra* or *Wolsdon* would tow the

Captain Jack Hocking, in his time with Reynolds' master of the tugs ALEXANDRA, CARBEILE *and* TACTFUL. *Jack transferred to Cory Ship Towage and when Corys finished at Plymouth, became a publican until retirement.*
JACK HOCKING

Antony back to the moorings before steam was raised again.

Danny Medway was mate firstly on the *Alexandra* and later on the *Trevol* with Captain Stan Bradford. He would sometimes take his wife Barbara out for trips and she recalled towing a large Royal Fleet Auxiliary ship (a dead ship going for scrap, no crew) out to the Sound and handing over to 'Sun' tugs from London. On another occasion she was aboard when in a gale the *Trevol* and *Tactful* had to go to Whitsand Bay, where a large US Navy ship was dragging her anchors and in danger of going ashore. The ship had to be held off the beach until steam could be raised and the engines started.

The long standing contract to dispose of the Dockyard refuse was more or less finished by 1965. The Dockyard Authorities wanted a more modern method of disposal, using skip lorries, with the refuse going to landfill. This would have required a hefty financial investment by Reynolds, one which they were not prepared to undertake, and eventually the contract was surrendered after over 80 years. English China Clays set up a subsidiary company named Haulwaste Ltd, bought new lorries, and the refuse was then tipped at a new landfill site at Chelson Meadow.

Over the years that Reynolds had the Dockyard contract it had been a mainstay of the firm, although it was not without various problems at times. The Admiralty Police would sometimes keep an eye on the hopper barges as it was not unknown for unscrupulous Dockyard employees to hide good materials under the refuse, in an effort to smuggle out timber and the like (there were always policemen on the Dockyard gates making sure that the men did not try to walk out with Government property). On one occasion an Admiralty policeman thought that some goods had been hidden in a hopper barge, and after the men had left one evening he was poking about in the barge trying to find the evidence, lifting up refuse and looking underneath when he lent over too far and fell into the barge on top of the refuse. He was rescued by a colleague after much shouting, with his uniform in less than pristine condition.

When one door closes another opens the saying goes and so it was the case for W. J. Reynolds Ltd. The South West Water Authority had decided to abandon as far as possible in the Plymouth area, the use of short sea outfalls for the disposal of raw sewage. They built three sewage treatment plants and the treated sewage was then to be taken to sea in barges and pumped out some distance offshore. This was a standard method of disposing of effluent at a number of locations around the country. It was usually undertaken by specialist ships, tankers that could discharge by pump or gravity when at sea. This practice occurred on the Thames, the Mersey, the Clyde, Belfast, Bristol, Exeter and many other ports. To seafarers and anybody with knowledge of ships and maritime matters, these vessels were generally known by the sobriquet 'Bovril Boats' as well as some other less printable names.

There were to be three loading points, at Camels Head, Hooe Lake and Plympton and W. J. Reynolds secured the contract to undertake the sea disposal. The old open hopper barges were not suitable, so four tank barges were purchased from the Thames. These barges were bought from Whiteways Cider and were towed down from London to Torpoint by a London tug. Reynolds modified the barges. On the Thames they had been loaded and emptied by shore installations, so Reynolds' engineers fitted a small deck house aft containing a large Gardner 6LW diesel engine which powered a pump. Suction pipes were installed into the tank bottoms.

Unlike the refuse contract where the barges would be moored alongside the Dockyard loading points and gradually filled, the sewage barges would be taken to the loading points and filled over the high water period in a fairly short time from shore storage. They were then towed straight away to the dumping ground (unless the weather was bad when the barges would be moored on the trot at Torpoint).

Left:
The concrete sewage loading tower in Hooe Lake.
Right:
The sewage loading tower on the river Plym at Marsh Mills
ALAN KITTRIDGE

The loading points at Camels Head and Hooe Lake were reasonably easily accessible but the Plympton one was not. In order to reach Plympton, a barge would be towed up towards Pomphlett by one of the big tugs and then handed over to the *Vussel* skippered by Billy Hocking, one of Jack Hocking's younger brothers and one of twins (the other twin Tony Hocking also worked for Reynolds and was a stoker, mainly on the *Tactful*). The barge would have to be towed up the River Plym under Laira Bridge. At low water most of the estuary above Laira Bridge dries out. Captain Archie Ayers remembered that Reynolds' men had marks on the bridge pillars from which they knew that when the water reached the mark on an incoming tide, there would be enough water for the little *Vussel* to set off towing the barge. She went with the flooding tide up to the loading point, which was situated where the wide mudflats finish and the river narrows, near the present A38 road bridge and Marsh Mills roundabout.

At Plympton because of the narrow river, it was essential to turn the barge around when it was in light (unloaded) state as the draft was only about three feet – when loaded the draft would be too deep to turn in the narrow river. The barge would be turned by running the bow ashore on the Plympton bank, swinging the stern around and then going alongside the loading point on her port side, facing downstream. The loading points at all three locations were not nice flat walled quays, but circular concrete towers with an iron ladder for access, and it was quite tricky to make fast and hold the barge alongside the towers. The mooring lines were permanently attached to moorings in the river bed either side of the tower and these had to be picked up with a grapple and made fast on the barge. Once this was done, the loading pipe from the tower would then be lowered over a hatch in the tank top of the barge, a valve opened and the barge loaded. Archie recalled that the loading arms were lifted and lowered by chain blocks, and even though the sewage treatment plants and loading quays were well fenced off, it was far from unknown to arrive at the loading point to find that the chain blocks had been stolen.

The smell from the treated sewage was, especially in the heat of the summer, far from pleasant and the crews were supplied with large drums of what was described as 'industrial strength Eau-de-Cologne' which was sprayed about with a hand held spray gun to try and mask the aroma.

The barge would be loaded by high water and as soon as the tide started to ebb the *Vussel* would set off back down under Laira Bridge to hand over to one of the bigger tugs, which would then tow the barge out to sea to dump. The bigger tugs could not of course pass under Laira Bridge, being too high. Archie said that the operation had to be carried out with the tide in each direction as the *Vussel* did not have the power to tow the barge against the tide. At Plympton loading could only take place around high water and on spring tides. On neap tides there was not enough depth of water so this meant that when the tides suited, sometimes two barges a tide might be loaded at Plympton to clear the holding tanks.

The *Vussel* would also be used to take barges to the loading tower in

Hooe Lake, where the tower stood (and still stands) in the middle of the lake. Once again there were moorings laid on the sea bed which had to be picked up on the approach. At busy times the *Vussel* would often take one barge up to Plympton and once the barge was secure alongside, race back down to Cattedown and pick up a second barge and take into Hooe. Whilst the second barge was loading the *Vussel* would go back to Plympton and bring the first barge back down, hand over to the steam tug and then return to Hooe for the second which would be towed out to Cattedown and handed to the tug. The larger tug would then set off with two barges in tow. If the weather was settled the tug would tow with one barge strapped on each side, which meant that the barge crews could ride out aboard the tug, but if the sea was too rough, then the barges would be towed astern on a long rope, and the barge crews would have to stay on the barges until the tug and barges returned to the shelter of the Breakwater on completion of dumping. Often both tides (there being two high waters every twenty four hours) would have to be worked with the crews working through the night as well, and the channel up the River Plym above Laira Bridge was specially buoyed for night working.

When the barges were being dumped at sea, some six miles seaward of Plymouth Breakwater, often small pieces of refuse could jam up the impellers on the pumps, and the crew on the barge would then have to dismantle the pump body to clear the blockage, with the inevitable spillage of the evil smelling cargo over the barge men.

The fleet on the trot at Torpoint:
CARBEILE, TACTFUL *and* TREVOL *with one of the sewerage barges moored midstream and the stern of the coaling barge on the right of the picture.*
DAVID MARTIN

A salvage job of which the details remain obscure, the TREVOL *(2) towing a heavily listing Turkish freighter from Cawsand Bay to the Sound on 4 February 1965.* W. J. REYNOLDS

CHAPTER ELEVEN

THE FINAL YEARS

A good salvage job turned up on 16 October 1967 when the Greek freighter *Arion* of 2,400 tons arrived in Plymouth Sound with generator problems. She anchored in Jennycliff Bay, but after a time the wind freshened from the south west, with gusts of over 50 miles per hour, and the ship started to drag her anchor towards the rocks. Plymouth lifeboat was launched and Reynolds' tugs: *Antony* - Captain Stan Bradford; and *Trevol* - Captain Steve Hannaford; rushed to the scene along with the Dockyard 'Dog' class tug *Alsatian*. When the coaster was within yards of going ashore, the *Antony* managed to get a line on board the bow of the ship and the *Alsatian* took hold aft, although the latter had to slip her line as she could not pull the stern up into the wind. The Greeks could not raise the anchor, as the windlass was electrically powered and the ship had no generator, so the *Antony* towed the ship, with her anchor still down, clear of the rocks and into deeper more sheltered waters on the west side of the Sound.

Saving the Greek ship ARION. TREVOL *(2) towing with the* ANTONY *(3) and the Dockyard tug* ALSATIAN *standing-by.*
W. J. REYNOLDS

Presentation to retiring Captain Stan Bradford, at the top of the ferry slip in Torpoint. The picture features from left to right: Danny Medway, David Callow, Reg Butson, Archie Ayers, Bert Furzland, Don Mead, Arthur Reynolds, Eric Martin, Tony Spiller (face obscured), Terry Metters, Stan Bradford, Jack Hocking, Alan Johnson, Reg Wiltshire, Ralf Farrell, and Steve Hannaford.
DAVID MARTIN

Less than a month later, on 9 November, the *Antony* had a less successful tow. The tug sailed to Dartmouth to pick up the ex-River Dart Steamboat Co's veteran paddle steamer, *Totnes Castle*, and in fine weather commenced to tow the paddler to Plymouth for scrapping. However the weather freshened and the sea became rough, the *Totnes Castle* started to take on water and eventually sank in 20 fathoms off Burgh Island.

Captain Steve Hannaford lived near Wares Quay in Saltash and is remembered as being very strong. He was born in Torpoint in 1910 and left school at 14 to join the merchant navy. In 1932 he came ashore from 'deep sea' and joined Reynolds. To get to work he owned a rowing skiff which he would row from Wares Quay to Torpoint, a distance of about two miles, and back home again when he had finished – winter and summer no matter what the weather was like. When Steve Hannaford became a little older, he bought a Kelvin petrol paraffin engined motor boat with which to commute to work, until he moved with his family to Torpoint and rented one of the many Reynolds' houses. Steve was appointed master in 1945 and served for a total of 43 years on the tugs, finishing up as master with Cory Ship Towage after they had taken over Reynolds. He was a keen oarsman and rowed for the Torpoint Rowing Club. One somewhat macabre trait was his habit of picking up bodies in the river. Often people would be drowned, either by accident or sometimes design, and as Steve Hannaford was travelling on the river at all hours of the day and night, on a number of occasions the bodies were recovered in his skiff or motorboat.

Captain Steve Hannaford (third from left), who was a noted oarsman, with a winning crew of the Torpoint Rowing Club.
GILL FERGUSON

Captain Hannaford would sometimes take his daughter Gillian with him on the tug until one day, aboard the *Trevol*, he was towing a ship out of Millbay Docks but the job did not go quite according to plan. The ship veered out of the channel and touched the bottom. The *Trevol* was pulled over at an alarming angle, and may have capsized had it not been for some quick engine movements. After that Steve would not take his daughter with him. He had also suffered a near miss in earlier times when he was mate – a tow rope parted under strain and whipped back and hit him; luckily he escaped with only cuts and bruises.

Arthur Reynolds, who had actually trained as a mining engineer, drove a big Jaguar motor car, very slowly. He was noted for driving around Torpoint at between 5 and 10 miles an hour. One day the car with Arthur driving was observed tearing through Torpoint at a great speed, a ship was in difficulties in the sound, the tugs had been dispatched and Arthur was hurrying to watch the operations from Rame Head.

It was his practice every morning to cross over on the chain ferry and call personally to see clients, like the Dockyard Superintendents, shipping agents, pilots, etc in Plymouth. Keeping this close contact was considered vital to maintaining the work of the firm. If the weather was nice, Arthur would occasionally take a trip out in the tugs taking his daughter Dinah with him. On one occasion the family dog Bimbo was on board but decided he didn't like the tug and jumped overboard to swim back towards Torpoint. The tide was strong and Bimbo was quickly swept seaward. He was lucky to be rescued by the crew of a Millbrook Steamboat Company pleasure boat, which was proceeding upstream with a party of trippers.

There were few signs of the firm nearing its end in 1968 – staff were still being taken on. Alan Harris was employed as a stoker, joining the *Carbeile* under engineer David Callow, and his brother, shipwright Peter Harris, joined the firm the following year, working under the foreman shipwright Fred Heard. Peter recalled working on maintenance aboard the tugs and barges, and also doing joinery work on the many properties, including 11 dwelling houses owned by the firm, mostly rented out to Reynolds' employees. Bill Cook was the engineer in charge at Carbeile Mill and Jack Dearden was in charge of the slipway.

Peter Harris also recalled that if a big ship was docking, the shore staff might be called upon to sail as extra crew on the tugs – mainly to help handling the tow ropes. Alan Harris would go down to keep the fires burning in a banked state over a weekend so that the tugs would be ready for Monday morning work (if they were not in use over the weekend), and for this he received an extra 10 shillings in his pay packet. When the tugs had been working down at Millbay or Cattedown and they were returning to Torpoint, Alan would start to clean and bank the fires when passing King Billy at Mutton Cove (King Billy is a figurehead of King William

TUG MAN QUITS AFTER 43 YEARS

After 43 years in the local tug fleet, Mr Stephen Hannaford, of Wesley Court, Torpoint, has retired.

Mr Hannaford, aged 65, joined the firm of W J Reynolds Ltd, in 1932 and was promoted Master in 1945. In 1972 the company was taken over by Cory Ship Towage Limited and Mr Hannaford continued serving them until his retirement on Thursday. A presentation ceremony is being arranged for next week when he will receive a stainless steel tea service from his shipmates.

The manager of the company at Torpoint, Mr Thomas Smith, who will be making the presentation, said Mr Hannaford had been an excellent tutor and his knowledge and experience would be greatly missed.

A local newspaper report on the retirement of Captain Steve Hannaford after 43 years service on Plymouth tugs.
GILL FERGUSON

Taken from the deck of the ANTONY *(3) bringing in the tanker* BRITISH OSPREY *with* CARBEILE *alongside and the funnel of the* TREVOL *which can just be made out to the left of the* CARBEILE's *funnel. The tow rope has a bridle or gog rope rigged. When the ship reached the turning ground off Turnchapel, the tanker would be swung through 180 degrees and the* TREVOL *would tow the ship up the Cattewater stern first. The* ANTONY *would then become the stern tug (although still on the bow of the ship) and the tow rope would be held down by the gog rope to prevent the tug being girted (capsized by the rope pulling at 90 degrees to the fore and aft line and dragging the tug sideways). In Plymouth this was known as being 'monkeyed down'.* DAVID MARTIN

TACTFUL (2) towing the Monrovian freighter IONIC COAST *into Fowey to load china clay. The indistinct tug on the ships bow is Fowey Harbour Commissioners first motor tug the* CANNIS. PAUL RICHARDS

IV, which has stood at Mutton Cove since 1860). This ensured that by the time the tug was moored up on the trot the steam pressure would be well down in the boiler. The fires would be banked with slack coal dowsed with water, the dampers on the boiler shut and the fires remained smouldering all night. The following morning the fires would be livened up, dampers opened and fresh coal put on and steam was up in no time. Alan Harris later stoked on the second *Tactful*, which he recalls could steam quickly as she had a steam powered fan in the boiler room. However, if the steam pressure was too low to operate the fan, then she would take an age to raise steam.

The *Wolsdon* and *Alexandra* were laid up and by 1970 both had been scrapped, leaving only the four larger steam tugs and the *Vussel* in the

TACTFUL (2) picking up a line from the CABLE RESTORER in Millbay Docks. RICHARD COX

TACTFUL (2) towing the cable ship CABLE RESTORER out of Millbay inner basin. RICHARD COX

Taken from the after deck of the TACTFUL (2) *whilst escorting the tanker* KOROVINA *to Cattedown Wharf. The* TACTFUL *is acting as third tug during swinging and berthing operations. Note the steam capstan fitted by Reynolds, for hauling down the bridle or gog rope. The crewman is stoker Tony Hocking, younger brother of the tug's Master, Captain Jack Hocking.*
MIKE DOHERTY

fleet. The loss of the Dockyard refuse contract probably made them redundant in any case. The *Alexandra*, acquired in the period of rampant inflation just after the Great War, was probably the most expensive tug purchased by Reynolds, but she proved to be an excellent investment, serving the firm for almost 50 years before being scrapped, and so became as well as the most expensive, the longest serving of all Reynolds' tugs.

What is thought to be the largest ship ever handled by Reynolds' tugs was the *Queen Frederica*, an elderly liner which the tugs assisted into the River Dart for lay up in 1971. The *Queen Frederica* was 582 feet long with a beam of 80 feet, a draft of 29 feet and was 21,329 gross tons. After an eight month stay on the Dart, the liner was assisted to sea again in 1972.

The end of the WOLSDON *in about 1967, alongside the scrap yard in Sutton Harbour.* DAVE HOCQUARD

The Cox built ANTONY *(3) being overhauled on the slipway at Carbeile.* J. AND M. CLARKSON

Around this time there was much talk of a brand new oil fired power station being built on the south side of St Johns Lake, with a deepwater channel being dredged so that large tankers could be brought in to supply the fuel. W. J. Reynolds' tugs were still in demand for ship handling in Plymouth, and they still had the South West Water Authority sewage contract. They still undertook the Eddystone relief (although the double ended pulling lifeboat had by this time been replaced by a motor launch the *Alert* owned by Trinity House), and still towed the 100 ton blocks out to the Breakwater.

By the start of 1972 Reynolds' fleet was an anachronism, all of the tugs being coal fired. Finding stokers who would put up with the work was becoming a problem and many of the men were, not to put too fine a point on it, as old as the tugs. The *Carbeile* and *Tactful* were still in excellent condition, but the *Trevol* had the pressure on her original 1921 boiler reduced, so lowering her power and it was feared a similar fate would soon befall the *Antony*.

It was, no doubt, Reynolds' sewage, Eddystone and Breakwater contracts, together with the prospect of large tankers at the proposed power station, which attracted the interest of Cory Ship Towage, who were aggressively expanding their business. Negotiations were opened in 1972 which resulted in Cory Ship Towage purchasing the good-will and contracts of W. J. Reynolds Ltd on 1 September 1972. The only vessels purchased by Cory's were the three tank barges used on the sewage contract. The remaining four tugs, *Antony, Carbeile, Tactful* and *Trevol* were taken on charter by Cory's for a short period until more modern motor tugs were transferred to Plymouth. The *Vussel* was also used for a short

The end: TREVOL, ANTONY, TACTFUL and CARBEILE still very much intact in 1977, after arriving under their own steam in 1972, at the scrap yard of Davies and Cann at Laira Bridge.
DAVE
HOCQUARD

period until Cory's purchased two Thames 'toshers', small barge tugs, from the London lighterage contractors W. J. Woodward Fisher. The four steam tugs were then sold for scrap, moving to the scrap yard of Davies and Cann at Laira Bridge, where they remained for nearly 15 years before being finally demolished.

Of the seagoing staff, some of the older men retired at the time of the takeover, but most of the others transferred to Cory Ship Towage.

The last vessel to operate commercially for W. J. Reynolds Ltd was the *Vussel*. Between 1971 and 1980 BBC Television made a long running series about a Victorian Liverpool ship owner, *The Onedin Line,* which starred Peter Gilmore as James Onedin. In a couple of episodes a steam boat was needed, and so the *Vussel* was 'converted' to look like an early Victorian steamer, and skippered during the filming by Billy Hocking dressed in Victorian costume. After becoming a film star the *Vussel* was laid up. Her eventual fate is not known, but she probably was left to rot and fell to pieces. It is somewhat ironic that W. J. Reynolds Ltd operated the very last fleet of coal fired steam tugs in the British

TURNCHAPEL MARINE

SEAVIEW QUAY

TURNCHAPEL

Phone : PLYMOUTH 42969

THE VUSSEL
Early 19th century Steam Pinnace which will be used
by the B.B.C. in the film
"THE ONEDIN LINE"
to be released next winter for Sunday evening viewing.
The vessel was prepared by Turnchapel Marine and is
correct, as far as is known, in every detail for this type
of craft of that period

**ANY TYPE OF WORK ON OLD OR NEW
BOATS UNDERTAKEN**
MOORINGS - DEEP WATER - SLIPWAY
CRANE - UNDER COVER WINTER STORAGE
Own Car Park
BRING YOUR PROBLEM TO US

Filming the ONEDIN LINE *at Dartmouth with the* VUSSEL *masquerading as an early Victorian steamer. The star of the series Peter Gilmore played James Onedin and is standing forward holding the mast. Billy Hocking, dressed in Victorian costume is in command.*
JILL WILTSHIRE

Cashing in on the ONEDIN LINE, *Turnchapel Marine who converted the* VUSSEL *placed this newspaper advertisement.*
JACK HOCKING

Isles, and the only motor vessel they ever owned was disguised as a steamer for television!

The slipway and Carbeile Mill engineering works continued doing outside work for a short time, with some of the staff kept on. It was hoped to find a buyer who would dredge out the creek and make a marina, but it was probably 10 years too soon. Eventually the slipway was sold to the Torpoint Slipping Company. The Mill and buildings were sold for development, as were the remaining farm lands. The Torpoint and District General Supply Co Ltd. buildings were sold to developers and the Ballast Pond was sold, eventually becoming the Torpoint Yacht Harbour. The reason for selling up, after three generations, was that none of the younger members of the family wanted to become involved, and both Art Reynolds and Reg Wiltshire were approaching retiring age.

W. J. Reynolds Ltd was formally wound up on 18 September 1973. At the time of winding up, the directors were Arthur Edward Reynolds, Secretary; and Reginald Trery Wiltshire J.P. The shareholders were the two directors and the Trustees of Wilfred John Reynolds; the Trustees of Archie Basil Reynolds; and Winifred Blanche Burleigh of Callington.

The WOLSDON took some time to disappear. The partially dismantled tug is still recognisable in 1977 after 10 years at the Sutton Harbour scrap berth.
DAVE HOCQUARD

August 1984 and some dismantling had taken place but the tugs are still fairly intact over 10 years after they finished with engines. DAVE HOCQUARD

The founder and his four sons, standing left to right: Fearnley Reynolds, William John Reynolds and Arthur Reynolds. Sitting left to right: Wilfred Reynolds and Claude Reynolds. JILL WILTSHIRE

Chapter twelve

The family

William John Reynolds was the eldest of eight children. He had six brothers and a sister. Some of his brothers also became prominent in the Torpoint business community: Thomas became a provision merchant and was a noted local preacher; Walter became a baker; Francis a plumber; and Albert a general dealer. In the early days they were able to help W. J. Reynolds by providing funds for the purchase of vessels by way of mortgages. At least two of William John's brothers served on the Torpoint Urban District Council, as did Major Reginald Wiltshire, later.

W. J. Reynolds and his wife Rebecca had four sons and a daughter. All the sons eventually entered the business but their daughter Cora Ernestine married Aubrey Williams and moved away from Torpoint. Family tradition suggests that the firm was sufficiently prosperous for the brothers to provide funds to their sister which enabled the Williams to live very comfortably with a full time maid. Of the third generation, only Arthur Edward Reynolds (son of Arthur Basil) took an active part in the business and he was joined by Reginald Wiltshire, who had married Betty

The 1905-6 Torpoint Association Football team with all four Reynolds brothers.
David Martin

TORPOINT ASSOCIATION FOOTBALL CLUB.

J. E. Coaker, W. Hayman, F. W. Roberts, A. Northcott, C. W. Reynolds, S. W. Tabb, E. Perry,
A. B. Reynolds,   *(Captain)*   W. J Reynolds,
(Hon. Sec.)   W. F. Reynolds. F. Prideaux. R. V. Goad. L. F. Selley, W. P. Coaker.   *(Hon. Treas.)*

Udalgarth, Torpoint, home of Arthur Reynolds and at one time the registered office of the company.
DAVID MARTIN

Reynolds' (daughter of Fearnley Reynolds). Fearnley himself remained actively involved in the company until his death in 1967. Wilfred Reynolds had one daughter, Winifred, who married Charles Burleigh and lived at Kelly Bray, Callington. On the death of her father she inherited her father's shares. Likewise, Claude Reynolds' only daughter, Monica, with his first wife Hilda (who died and he remarried) married Cecil Martin and inherited her father's shares.

The only member of the family still living at Torpoint at the time of writing is Dinah Reynolds, daughter of Arthur Edward Reynolds, the other descendants having spread far and wide.

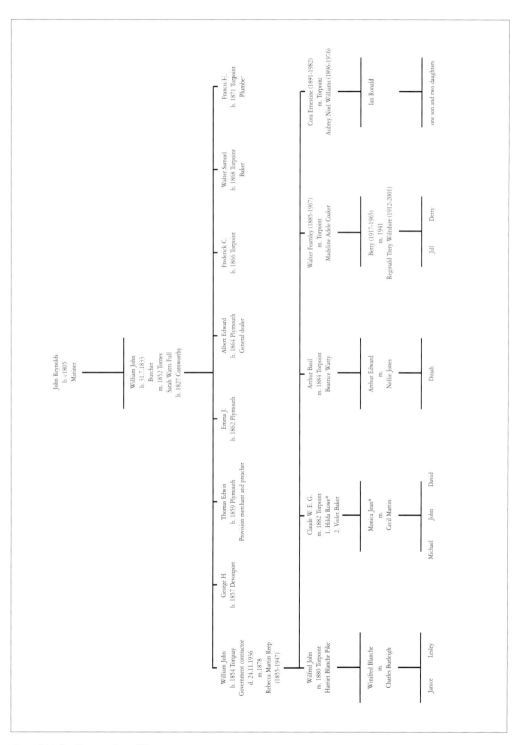

Reynolds' family tree. JILL WILTSHIRE

A Torpoint and District General Supply Co horse and cart being decorated for a carnival or agricultural show. Standing by the cart is Jack Dawe, the farm manager, Harry Pearce and the horse is ROYAL.
DINAH REYNOLDS

CHAPTER THIRTEEN
HORSES

Until the last 20 years, heavy horses were an integral part of the Reynolds business. The horses worked the farm fields, pulled the coal delivery carts for the domestic coal deliveries of the General Supply Co, delivered building materials and agricultural supplies, pulled the carts to bunker the Torpoint Ferries and of course pulled the tipping carts within the Dockyards collecting the ashes and rubbish and transporting this waste to the hopper barges.

Jack Dawe harrowing at the Mill Farm, with Carbeile Road in the background. The horses are (left to right): ROYAL, CAPTAIN *and* TIGER.
DAVID MARTIN

In W J Reynolds day-book, there are far more entries regarding the purchase of horses, purchase of fodder, repairs to harness and incidents involving horses than there are about the tugs and barges. In the main, most of the horses were of the two staple British draught horse breeds, Shires and Clydesdales.

Only belatedly, and one feels with some reluctance, did the firm eventually phase out horse power in favour of motor transport.

Reynolds' biggest heavy horse, the 18 hand stallion KING *with a Torpoint and District General Supply Co four wheel cart.*
DAVID MARTIN

The two Cory ship handling tugs that replaced Reynolds' steamers, FALGARTH *and* PLYMGARTH.
DAVE HOCQUARD

Postscript

Cory Ship Towage introduced two diesel ship handling tugs, the *Falgarth* and *Plymgarth* with two small barge tugs *Torgarth* and *Tregarth*. However a declining workload and the loss of the South West Water Authority sewage contract to civil engineering contractors Dean and Dyball Ltd, caused the closure of the Plymouth operation in 1989.

Cory barge tug TORGARTH *(above)* AND TREGARTH *(below)* towing, alongside, one of the four sewage barges. DAVE HOCQUARD

Carbeile Mill is now a boatyard, and the Ballast Pond is a yacht harbour. The premises of the Torpoint and District General Supply Co have been redeveloped. The patent cradle slipway ceased trading and was removed – the site of the top of the slipway now being occupied by two bungalows. Many of the commercial quays and wharfs where Reynolds' tugs would assist shipping have changed. The inner basin at Millbay Docks has been partially filled in, and Sutton Harbour is now, largely, a marina. The original stone loading facilities at Pomphlett have been

125

The builders plate of the tug BAHIA.

replaced by a boatyard as have the berths at Prince Rock and Laira Wharf.

The last surviving director, Reg Wiltshire died in 2001. His funeral service was conducted at Maryfield Church, Antony, where he had married Betty Reynolds many years before. (The service being conducted by the Reverend Christine Musser who later gained fame on television as the Vicar of Boscastle.) Virtually nothing remains of the tugs, Jill Wiltshire has the ships bell of the *Alexandra* whilst the bell of the *Carbeile* (still engraved as *George Livesey*) is used to call time at the Torpoint Rowing Club at the top of the ferry beach at Torpoint.

The firm who in their day were the largest employer of civilian labour in Torpoint, and who for 90 years kept many families well provided for, is now all but forgotten.

Reynold's tugs on the trot off Torpoint. A once familiar view.

Pages from a W. J. Reynolds' tide table booklet for 1971.
DAVID MARTIN

TUG SIGNALS BY WHISTLE.

One Blast, **Wheel and Ship's Head to Starboard**

Two Blasts, **Wheel and Ship's Head to Port**

Three Blasts, **Shorten in Tow Rope**

One Short and Two Long Blasts
Let go Tow Rope

With Compliments
from

W. J. Reynolds, Ltd.
Tug Owners
Torpoint

RECOGNISED CALL
FOR TUGS—
One Long and Two Short Blasts

W. J. Reynolds' fleet list
chronological order

Bessie
Steam launch details unknown.

Dainty
Wood, steam passenger launch built 1881 by Simpson Strickland, Dartmouth.
37 x 8 x 3 feet. 7.95 GRT. Engine: 2 cylinder compound of 6 NHP. Broken up 1903.

Link
Wood, steam passenger launch built 1883 by Simpson Strickland, Dartmouth.
42 x 9 x 4 feet. 10 GRT. Engine: by builders, 2 cylinder compound 6 NHP. Broken up
1903.

Marguerite
Iron, steam paddle passenger steamer. Built London 1879 for the London
Metropolitan Asylums Board as a river ambulance. Subsequently owned by various
Thames passenger boat operators. Reynolds purchased her from W. J. Harse of
Oxford. 69 x 10 x 4 feet. 23 GRT. Engine: 10 NHP sold by 1903.

Lorna
Iron, steamer (tug) built Plymouth 1875. Purchased by Reynolds c.1903 from Frank
Philips of the Barbican, Plymouth. 44 x 8.5 x 5 feet. 13 GRT. Engine: single cylinder
12 NHP. Out of use and broken up by 1919.

Mascotte
Wood, steam launch built Plymouth by Isaac Darton in 1882. 39 x 8 x 5 feet.
10 GRT. Engine: compound 6 NHP 25 IHP by Alexander Wilson, London, cylinders
6 ins and 12 ins by 7 ins stroke. Boiler 120psi. Broken up 1919.

Saxon
Iron, tug built Cox and Co Falmouth 1883. Owners Joseph and Henry Cox,
Falmouth. 1889 sold to Walter Arthur, Newport Monmouthshire. 1894 supposedly
sold to Norwegian owners but deal fell through and then sold to William Rowe,
Falmouth. Purchased by W. J. Reynolds 1911. 58 x 10 x 6 feet. 24 GRT engine by
Cox 14 NHP 90 IHP, 2 cylinder compound. Scrapped 1928.

Briton
Wood, tug built 1905 Falmouth by W H Lean for William Rowe, Falmouth.
Purchased by W. J. Reynolds 1913. 68 x 14 x 3 feet. 40 GRT. Engines by Cox and
Co 24 NHP 210 IHP, 2 cylinder compound. Broken up by 1950.

Alexandra
Steel, passenger carrying tug built 1902 by Cox and Co Falmouth for the St Mawes
Steam Tug and Passenger Co. Purchased by W. J. Reynolds 1919. 84.6 x 16.9 x 7.7
feet. 73 GRT. Engines by Cox, 3 cylinder triple expansion 50 NHP 300 IHP, new
boiler 1949. Laid up by 1968 and scrapped by 1970.

Scraesdon
Iron, tug built 1881 by Michot, Belgium as the *Leopold I* for SARH-SA de
Remorquage a Helice, Antwerpen. 1905 sold to George F. Treleaven, Plymouth,
purchased by W. J. Reynolds 1920. 72.7 x 16 x 8.1 feet. 65 GRT. Engine 2 cylinder
30 NHP 180 IHP by Ateliers and Constructions Bonsan (Belgium). Broken up by
1929.

Boarhound
Iron, tug built 1881 by Michot (Belgium) as the *Leopold II* for SARH-SA de Remorquage a Helice at Antwerpen. 1905 sold to George F. Treleaven, Plymouth, re- engined and re-named *Boarhound*. 1920 purchased by W. J. Reynolds. 73.2 x 16 x 8.1 feet. 65 GRT. Engines 24 NHP 130 IHP. Re-engined and re-boiled in 1905, boiler by Rileys of Stockton, engine Willoughby Bros Plymouth. 24 NHP 200 IHP, cylinders 12 ins and 24 ins by 16 ins stroke. Out of use by 1955 and broken up by 1963.

Wolsdon
Steel, tug built 1896 in London as the *Eagle* for the War Office. Based at Devonport and mainly used for target towing. 1926 purchased by W. J. Reynolds and renamed *Wolsdon*. 60.2 x 13.3 x 5.6 feet. 36 GRT 24 NHP 190 IHP. Out of service by 1969 and scrapped by 1970.

Antony (1)
Steel, tug built Philip and Sons Dartmouth 1917 as the *HS29* for the War Office. 1921 to Crichton Thompson and Co, London. Purchased by W. J. Reynolds 1926 and renamed *Antony*. Sold in 1928 to the Shipowners Towage Syndicate, Antwerpen and renamed *Cooperator*. 85.5 x 22.1 x 9.0 feet. 144 GRT 45 NHP 500 IHP. 2 cylinder compound engine.

Trevol (1)
Steel, tug built Hawthorn, Leith in 1917 as the *HS28* for the War Office (but could well have been built by Philips Dartmouth, see text chapter 4). 1921 to Crichton Thompson and Co, London. Purchased by W. J. Reynolds 1926 and renamed *Trevol*. 85.5 x 22.1 x 9.0 feet. 136 GRT. 43 NHP 450 IHP. 2 cylinder compound engine, cylinders 15 ins and 32 ins x 24 ins stroke. Boiler 150psi 10.5 feet long, 13.5 feet diameter. Out of service by 1956 and scrapped by 1960.

HS30
Steel, screw tug built 1917 by J. Cran, Leith for the War Office. 1921 to Critchton Thompson Co, London. Purchased by W. J. Reynolds in 1926 sold without renaming to the Manchester Ship Canal Co. Renamed *Mount Manisty*. 85 x 21 x 10.5 feet. 154 GRT 87 NHP 500 IHP

HS31
Steel, screw tug built 1917 by J. Cran, Leith for the War Office. 1921 to Crichton Thompson Co, London. Purchased by W. J. Reynolds in 1926 sold without renaming to the Manchester Ship Canal Co. Renamed *Cadishead*. 85 x 21 x 10.5 feet. 154 GRT. 87 NHP 500 IHP.

Cruden Bay
Wood, screw tug built by William Jarvis, Anstruther in 1899 as a fish carrier/trawler. 97 x 20 x 10 feet. 124 GRT. Engine and boiler built J. Cran, Leith, 2 cylinder compound with cylinders 12 ins and 30 ins by 20 ins stroke. 47 NHP 210 IHP. Purchased by W. J. Reynolds Ltd for spares only in 1928. Never registered to W. J. Reynolds. Gradually dismantled at Carbeile Creek.

Hasty
Steel, mining vessel (mine layer). Built Hawthorn, Leith 1891 as the *Napier of Magdala* for the War Department. Renamed *Linnet* in 1906 and *Hasty* in 1913. According to W. J. Reynolds records purchased 26 February 1931 but according to Admiralty records sold to W. J. Reynolds 20 February 1932. 80 x 18 feet. 144 GRT. Purchased for spares only and not used.

HS35
Steel, single screw tug built by Hawthorn, Leith for the War Office. 1921 to
Crichton Thompson Co, London. Purchased by W. J. Reynolds (or the family
privately) about 1931 (dates not confirmed). Sold to unknown purchaser without
entering Reynolds' fleet. 85 x 21 x 10.5 feet. 154 GRT. 87 NHP 450 IHP

Antony (2)
Steel, screw tug built Hepple and Co, South Shields in 1902 as the *Commonwealth* for
the Empire Towing Company, Gravesend. Purchased by Gamecock Steam Towing
Co Gravesend. From 1914 to 1919 on Admiralty War Office service as the
Commonweal. Then owned successively by the British India Steam Navigation Co
Ltd, London; and the United Steam Tug Co, Gravesend. Resumed original name,
and sold in 1931 to Sydney Charles Roberts and L. Vandeventer (Commonwealth
Steam Tug Co) Bristol. Purchased by W. J. Reynolds in 1934 and renamed *Antony*.
90.7 x 19.6 x 10.8 feet. 115 GRT. 98 NHP 585 IHP compound engine, cylinders 18
ins and 38 ins x 25 ins stroke. Broken up at Carbeile Mill 1960.

Bahia
Steel, screw tug built Day Summers and Co, Southampton in 1907 for Wilson and
Sons of London (but for operation in Brazil). In 1923 purchased by Captain Stephen
A. Portus of Garston. In 1930 passed to James Dredging, Towage and Transport Co
Ltd, Southampton. Purchased by W. J. Reynolds in 1935. 80.3 x 16.3 x 8.4 feet.
85 GRT. 350 IHP. By 1955. Dismantled at Carbeile Mill scrapped by 1963.

Tactful (1)
Steel, screw tug built J. Fullerton and Co Paisley as the *Lord Beresford* for the
Maritime Dredging and Construction Co of St Johns, New Brunswick Canada.
Purchased by the War Office in 1917 and renamed *HS71*. Transferred to the
Admiralty in 1919 as the *Lord Beresford*. Sold to W. Shelcott and Sons, London 1920
and the same year to Charles Etheridge London, renamed *Tactful*. Sold to the Great
Yarmouth Steam Tug Co 1927. Purchased by W. J. Reynolds Ltd in 1938. 75.2 x
18.6 x 8.9 feet. 112 GRT.. 46 NHP 400 IHP. Engine 2 cylinder compound, cylinders
14 ins and 28 ins by 24 ins stroke. Scrapped in Sutton Pool, Plymouth 1964.

Vussel
Wooden, pinnace about 42 feet long. Double diagonal construction. Purchased from
the Admiralty in the 1930s and fitted with welding plant and burning gear as a
floating workshop. After the Second World War the launch was converted by W. J.
Reynolds by fitting a petrol/paraffin engine. Later engine changed for a Kelvin K4
diesel. 88 BHP. Used on the filming of the *Onedin Line* TV series. Eventual fate
unknown.

Trethosa
Steel, screw tug built Smit and Zoon, Kinderdijk, Holland 1884 for William
Watkins Ltd, London. Sold 1885 to Cowes Steam Tug Co. Sold 1890 to Queenstown
Screw Tug and Ship Co, Cork. Sold 1902 to the Liverpool Screw Towing and
Lighterage Co Ltd, Liverpool, renamed *Fighting Cock*. Sold 1947 to Toyne Carter and
Co Fowey, renamed *Trethosa*. Sold 1947 to the Fowey Tug Co Ltd. Purchased by W.
J. Reynolds Ltd 1949. 97.9 x 19.1 x 11.4 feet. 119 GRT. Engine 2 cylinder
compound 80 NHP 300 later 600 IHP by Charles Burrell and Sons, Thetford,
Norfolk. Cylinders 20 ins and 40 ins x 24 ins stroke. Boiler 10 feet long 11.5 feet
diameter. Vessel scrapped by Demmelweek and Redding in Sutton Pool 1963.

Gallant
Iron, screw tug built Rother Ironworks, Rye in 1884 for Ernest Chaplin and others
for use at Fowey. Lengthened 1903. Various owners, managed by Fowey Tug and
Salvage Co and Fowey Tug Co (Henry A. Paull). Sold 1946 to Toyne Carter and Co
Fowey. Sold 1948 to the Fowey Tug Co Ltd. Sold 1951 to Fowey Harbour

Commissioners. Purchased by W. J. Reynolds in 1954. As built 77 x 16 x 9 feet. 69 GRT. Lengthened 1903 to be 86 x 16 x 9 feet and tonnage increased to 76 GRT.. Engine 2 cylinder compound by the builders, 38 NHP 300 IHP, cylinders 16 ins and 30 ins x 20 ins stroke. Scrapped by Demmelweek and Redding in Sutton Pool 1963.

Carbeile
Steel, screw tug built by Lytham Shipbuilding and Engineering Co Ltd in 1929 as the *George Livesey* for the South Metropolitan Gas Company, London. 1949 owners restyled as South Eastern Gas Board, London. Purchased by W. J. Reynolds Ltd 1957. 77.6 x 21.6 x 10.6 feet. 110 GRT. Engines by builder triple expansion 44 NHP 550 IHP with cylinders 14 ins, 22 ins and 36 ins by 24 ins stroke. Boiler originally designed to burn coke. Displacement 196 tons. Sold to Davies and Cann Laira Bridge, Plymstock for scrapping in 1973. Not broken up until 1984 (register closed 1979, vessel no longer navigable).

Antony (3)
Steel, screw tug Built Cox and Co, Falmouth in 1921 as the *Corgarth* for R. and J. H. Rea Ltd, Bristol. Purchased by W. J. Reynolds Ltd 1960 and renamed *Antony*. 84.1 x 21.8 x 11.5 feet. 137 GRT. Engines by builder triple expansion 91 NHP 650 IHP with cylinders 14.5 ins, 22 ins and 36 ins by 24 ins stroke. Boiler pressure 180psi. Displacement 247 tons. Vessel sold 1973 to Davies and Cann, Laira Bridge for scrapping. Finally demolished by 1984. (register closed 1979 vessel no longer navigable).

Trevol (2)
Steel, screw tug Built Cox and Co, Falmouth in 1921 as the *Reagarth* for R. and J. H. Rea Ltd, Bristol. Purchased by W. J. Reynolds Ltd in 1962 and re named *Trevol*. 84.1 x 21.8 x 11.5 feet. 137 GRT. Engines by builder triple expansion 91 NHP 650 IHP with cylinders 14.5 ins, 22 ins and 36 ins by 24 ins stroke. Boiler pressure 180psi. Displacement 247 tons. Vessel sold 1973 to Davies and Cann, Laira Bridge for scrapping. Finally demolished by 1984. (register closed 1979, vessel no longer navigable).

Tactful (2)
Steel, screw tug. Built 1928 by Fellows and Go, Great Yarmouth as the *F T Everard* for F. T. Everard and Sons Ltd, Greenhithe, Kent. Sold 1951 to Fowey Tug Co Ltd and renamed *Tolbenny*. Sold 1961 to Fowey Harbour Commissioners. Purchased by W. J. Reynolds Ltd in 1965 and renamed *Tactful*. 83.0 x 21.6 x 11.0 feet. 124 GRT. Engines by builder, triple expansion 102 NHP 550 IHP with cylinders 13.5 ins, 22 ins and 36 ins by 27 ins stroke. Forced draught fan in boiler room. Vessel sold 1973 to Davies and Cann at Laira Bridge for scrapping. Finally demolished by 1984. (Register closed 1979, vessel no longer navigable).

BARGE FLEET

Jumbo
Iron, hopper barge. Built Portsmouth 1889. Purchased by W. J. Reynolds and Samuel Hugh Duff in 1909. Still listed as owned by Reynolds in 1953. 86 x 21 x 5.5 feet. 71 GRT.

Tap
Iron, hopper barge. Built Portsmouth 1888. Purchased by W. J. Reynolds and Samuel Hugh Duff in 1909. Still in service in 1960. 86 x 22 x 6 feet. 81 GRT.

Thames
Iron, hopper barge. Owned prior to 1911 other details not known.

Yank
Steel, hopper barge

Jubilee
Iron, hopper barge purchased by W. J. Reynolds in 1914.

FHC No 2
Wooden, hopper barge built by J Dibble and Sons, Southampton in 1912. Purchased by W. J. Reynolds in about 1925. 98.7 x 25.2 x 7.1 feet. 137 GRT.

FHC No 4
Wooden, hopper barge purchased by W. J. Reynolds in 1935 107 GRT.

Clearwell
Steel, hopper barge built Leith in 1927. Purchased by W. J. Reynolds in 1939. 95 x 23 x 7.5 feet. 139 GRT.

Claretta
Wooden, hopper barge owned by Plymouth Corporation. Purchased by W. J. Reynolds 1931.

Brook
Hopper barge.

Test
Coaling barge.

Start Point
Steel, Thames swim head tank lighter. Converted for sewage disposal. Approximately 250 tons capacity. Gardner engine driven sewage pumps.

Stone Bow
as above

Torpoint
as above.

There were certainly other barges owned at times but details have not survived.

LIVERY

For the most part Reynolds' tugs had a black hull with either a white or yellow band at deck level. During the 1930s the hulls were painted battleship grey between the waterline and the deck.

The boiler room and engine casings were usually a light brown colour. Wheelhouses were either varnished or light brown bottom with a white top, and the funnels were buff (almost yellow on some occasions) with a black top.

The colour scheme certainly varied over the years and no doubt was influenced by whatever paint may have been disposed of by Devonport Dockyard.

Executed in Nine pages.

D & O 7.

ISSUED BY THE BOARD OF TRADE.

10 JAN

OFFICIAL LOG-BOOK

AND

LIST OF THE CREW

OF A SHIP OF LESS THAN 80 TONS REGISTER EXCLUSIVELY
EMPLOYED UPON THE COASTS OF THE UNITED KINGDOM AND EIRE.

Name of Ship.	Official Number.	Port No. and Port of Registry.	Tonnage. Gross.	Net.	Horse Power.	Date of Commencement of Half-Year.	Date of Termination of Half-year.
ANTONY	115916	Plymouth	114.84	49.585	98 NHP	1. 7. 40	31·12·40

REGISTERED MANAGING OWNER OR MANAGER.

Name.	Address. (State No. of House, Street and Town.)
Los Reynolds Ltd	Coryton House Torpoint Cornwall

MASTER.

Name and No. of Certificate (if any).	Address. (State No. of House, Street and Town.)
S. Bradford	6. Alexandra Terrace Torpoint

To be filled in by the Master at the end of the last voyage or the Half-year.

I hereby declare to the truth of the entries in this official log-book and list of the crew.

S Bradford ....Master.

To be filled in by the Superintendent.

Received at.................. the...................day of...................19......

M.M. OFFICE
9 JAN 1941
PLYMOUTH

Abacombe

{ Superintendent of a
{ Mercantile Marine Office.

LIST OF THE CREW

The names, &c., of ALL the seamen (including young persons, but excluding any seaman under

Reference No.	Names of the MASTER and the Crew.	Year of Birth.	† Nationality. (If British, state birthplace.)	Ship in which he last served and Port to which she belonged.	Year of Service in last Ship.
		2	3	4	5
1	Master. S. Bradford	1904	all British Torpoint	Save Employ	1910
2	R. Butson	1910	"	"	"
3	S. Hannaford	1909	"	"	"
4	L. Lewis	1889	Looe	"	"
5	S. Cox	1887	"	"	"
6	W. Knott	1912	Torpoint	"	"
7	C. Cobb	1905	"	"	"
8	E. Cobb	1881	St Peren	"	"
9					
10					
11					
12					
13					
14					
15					

REGISTER OF YOUNG PERSONS UNDER THE AGE

Name in full.	Date of Birth.	† Nationality. (If British, state birthplace.)	In what Capacity engaged.	Date of joining this Ship during the half-year.

* PARTICULARS of all BIRTHS on Board during the Half-year.

Date of Birth.	Name (if any) of Child.	Sex.	Name and Surname of Father.	Rank, Profession, or Occupation of Father.	Name and Surname of Mother.	Maiden Surname of Mother.

*PARTICULARS of all DEATHS on Board during the Half-year.

Date of Death.	Place of Death.	Name and Surname of Deceased.	Sex.	Age.	Crew or Passenger.	Rank or Rating, Profession or Occupation.

† If a British subject, state town or country of birth, and if born in a

* See Directions on ·

Crew list of the ANTONY (2) for the second half of 1940. Captain Stan Bradford, engineer Reg Butson and mate Steve Hannaford. DAVE BRADFORD

This Indenture made the _TWELFTH._

day of _NOVEMBER._ One thousand nine hundred and _FIFTY SIX._

BETWEEN _ROY. LIONEL WILLIAM. MORGAN._

of _ST. LEONARD'S CARBEAL. ROAD. TORPOINT. CORNWALL_

(hereinafter called " the Parent ") of the first part

MICHAEL WILLIAM MORGAN. aged _15_ years _9 m._

son of the said _Roy Lionel William Morgan_

(hereinafter called " the Apprentice ") of the second part

and _W. J. REYNOLDS LTD. ENGINEERS & SHIP. REPAIRERS._
of _CORYTON HOUSE TORPOINT. CORNWALL._

(hereinafter called " the Employer ") of the third part

WITNESSETH as follows that is to say :

1. The Apprentice of his own free will and with the consent and approbation of the Parent (testified by his execution of this Deed) hereby binds himself to serve the Employer as his Apprentice in his art, trade or business of _ENGINE FITTER & TURNER._ for the term of _FIVE_ years from the _TWELFTH_ day of _NOVEMBER_ One thousand nine hundred and _FIFTY SIX._

Delete as necessary

2. In consideration of the [services of the Apprentice] [sum of paid to the Employer by the Parent (the receipt whereof the Employer hereby acknowledges)] the Employer hereby covenants with the Parent and the Apprentice and each of them severally as follows :

   (a) That he will accept the Apprentice as his Apprentice during the said term and will during the said term to the best of his power skill and knowledge instruct the Apprentice or cause him to be instructed in all branches of his art trade or business as aforesaid now carried on by him at

   and in all things incidental or relating thereto

   (b) That he will pay to the Apprentice during the said term the wages set out in the Schedule hereto

3. In consideration of the premises the Parent (for himself his Executors and Administrators) and the Apprentice hereby severally covenant with the Employer as follows :

   (a) That the Apprentice shall truly and faithfully during the said term serve the Employer as his Apprentice in his said art trade or business of

AT. TORPOINT &

   at _MARINE ENGINEERING FITTING & TURNING_ aforesaid and at any other place where he may at any time during the said term carry on the same

   (b) That the Apprentice shall diligently attend to the said business his Employer's secrets keep and at all times willingly obey the lawful commands of the Employer and others having authority over him during the said term

   (c) That the Apprentice shall not absent himself from the Employer's service without the leave of the Employer

   (d) That the Apprentice shall not do or knowingly suffer to be done any damage to the Employer or to the goods or moneys or other things which shall be put in his custody or care and shall not embezzle or waste them or lend or dispose of them to any one without the Employer's consent

   (e) That the Apprentice shall not gamble with cards or dice or play at unlawful games or frequent taverns but that in all things he shall demean and behave himself towards his Employer and others having authority over him during the said term as a good and faithful apprentice ought

   (f) That the Parent will during the said term provide the Apprentice with good and sufficient board and lodging wearing apparel medical attendance and medicine (so far as not furnished by the State) and all other necessaries

(*g*) If the Apprentice shall at any time be guilty of any act or omission contrary to or in breach of the covenants hereinbefore contained the Parent shall pay to the Employer the sum of
as and by way of liquidated damages and not as a penalty

4. PROVIDED ALWAYS and IT IS HEREBY AGREED AND DECLARED as follows :

(*a*) The Employer shall not be entitled to make any deduction from the said wages in respect of the usual holidays or any other holidays from time to time allowed by the Employer to the Apprentice but the Apprentice shall not be entitled to any wages if and while he is absent from work through illness or other incapacity or through his own default and the Employer shall be entitled to deduct from the said wages a part proportionate to the number of working hours lost through such absence and also any sum or sums which may be reasonable for any loss which the Employer may sustain by reason of the negligence or misconduct of the Apprentice

(*b*) If the Apprentice shall at any time during the said term wilfully disobey the lawful orders or command of the Employer or others having authority over him during the said term or be slothful or negligent or shall otherwise grossly misbehave himself towards the Employer or others having authority over him then and in any such case it shall be lawful for the Employer to discharge the Apprentice from his service (provided that in such case the Employer shall repay to the Parent the sum of for every complete year of the said term which shall then be unexpired) and thereupon these presents shall become void for all purposes save for the purpose of enforcing payment of damages under and by virtue of the covenant of the Parent hereinbefore contained

Delete if no premium has been paid by the Parent.

(*c*) If the provisions of this Deed are duly complied with by the Apprentice this Deed shall be delivered to the Apprentice on the completion of the said term of apprenticeship with a Certificate of such service endorsed thereon

IN WITNESS whereof the parties hereto have hereunto set their hands and seals the day and year first before written

THE SCHEDULE before referred to :

The wages of the Apprentice during the said term shall be as follows :—

For the First year	56/7.	WEEKLY
For the Second year	66/7.	"
For the Third year	90/4	"
For the Fourth year	106/10	"
For the Fifth year	127/-	"
For the Sixth year		
For the Seventh year		

SIGNED SEALED and DELIVERED by
the said
(the Parent) in the presence of   *Roy. Lionel William Morgan.*

SIGNED SEALED and DELIVERED by
the said
(the Apprentice) in the presence of   *Michael. William. Morgan.*

SIGNED SEALED and DELIVERED by
the said
(the Employer) in the presence of   *A.B. Reynolds.*

DIRECTOR
W. J. REYNOLDS LTD.

I hereby certify that the hereinbefore named
MICHAEL WILLIAM MORGAN
has well and faithfully served the full period of his Apprenticeship in accordance with the terms of the before written Deed

Dated this *5th* day of *February.*
One thousand nine hundred and *Sixty-Two.*

W J Reynolds
Director.

Michael Morgan's indentures. MICHAEL MORGAN

W. J. REYNOLDS LTD.

ENGINEERS, SHIP REPAIRERS
& TUG OWNERS

TORPOINT, CORNWALL.

This is to Certify *that* _____
has completed a term of _____ *years as* _____
Apprentice _____

Given under our hands this _____ *day of*
_____ *Nineteen hundred and* _____

S

_____ DIRECTOR
_____ DIRECTOR
_____ SECRETARY

W. J. Reynolds Ltd., certificate of completion of indentures. JILL WILTSHIRE

The MATCH of the SEASON
MILL HOTSPURS Versus THE MARINERS

Christmas Day 1935
Sunderland and the Arsenal would lose by 6 to nil
If they, in Cup Ties had to meet the Hotspurs of the Mill;
The men of Thankes are clever, they can dribble, pass and shoot
And the Cornish Junior Championship is held by the Institute,
The lads of St. James are noted for sportsmanship and skill,
But all these teams rank far below the Hotspurs of the Mill.
Some of the Spurs are horsemen and train on oats and bran
With many a dish of chicken meal prepared by Trainer Dan
Some of them at Tamar Wharf handle the timber and coal
And a veteran international is the guardian of their goal.
A seagull left the Ballast Pond and flew across the Sound
To meet the men of the towing fleet as they were homeward bound;
He told the news to the Skipper early on Christmas Day
He, and his merry hoppers a football match must play.
'Boys' said the ancient mariner who had passed the Head of Rame,
'Friend Drake defeated landsmen and we will do the same;
we will beat the 'Tamar Wharfers' and make them homeward fly,
And put Dan and his horsemen with the porkers in the sty.
The men who drove the lorries or work with Foreman Leach,
We will stow them in a hopper and sink them out of reach.
Our hears [sic] are acetylene welded and hardened on a forge
And we will go in training 'neath the loving care of George.

There was no lack of excitement when the teams lined out to play
A game of all-in football on the morn of Christmas Day.
All the Boss-hands attended this rare good sport to see,
Admiral Fearn was a linesman and Claude the referee;
Young Arthur the other linesman must many lessons learn
Ere he enters football circles with Uncles Claude and Fearn.
Amongst the distinguished guests were players of years ago,
Foreman Leach and Avent Bill had Fennington Jack in tow,
One had come prepared to lubricate his throttle
And no doubt others shared a wee drop from the bottle.

While the Admiral did his touch line sprints between the netted poles
He dreampt of a Cornish Final when he scored a brace of goals.
He lost his sea legs often when pacing Fuzzy Hany
And Fearn was obliged on Boxing Day a walking stick to carry.

Here are the names of the players so youthful, bold and fierce,
Southard 'kept' the Mariners goal, in the other was Harry Pierce.
Raglan and one of the Butsons were the backs of the Towing Fleet.
While Dasher Rice and Clements saved the landsmen from defeat.
Hannaford, Squance and Devereaux Bill were the Mariners brilliant halves
The landsmen had Heales with Knott and Cook a trio with shapely calves.
Willcocks led the Fleet attack and bravely he did the job
With him were the Fuzzy brothers, Devereaux (Dick) and Lobb.
The forward line of the landsmen with anything could contend'
They were Tamblin, Tickle and Butson, Dicky Pierce and Friend.

The referee gave the signal and away on a westward tack
Went the light and speedy Mariners with their pilot Willcocks Jack.
He beat young Albert by a Knott and gave the ball a flick,
It flew away to the touchline to knock out Devereaux Dick;
The slim and nimble outside right was thinking of his dinner
And begged the trainer to be relieved by a featherweight Richard Skinner.
But George the trainer answered 'You must stay there to the close.
And should you score the winning goal you shall have the parsons nose.'

The venue of the play was changed and Raglan got in a pickle
When Tamblin robbed him of the ball and passed it on to Tickle.
Southard had to play around his goal net to defend
From shots by Butson (Leslie) Dicky Pearce and Friend.
But at length the Mariner Butson to his keeper brought relief
As he punted to Fuzzy Harry who quickly came to grief.
He seemed to lose his sea legs and soon became a wreck
When in collision with Dasher he fell upon the 'deck',
'But sailors don't care' so Harry can take a few hard knocks
And again he sailed on a level keel with trousers inside his socks.
Clements kicked to Devereaux Bill who steered the ball to port
But Cook its course diverted and sent it to Southard's fort.
Harry had many lessons taught by brother Bert
But often seeking for the ball he made a fruitless spurt;
Thus up and down the field they went, there was no chance to tarry
And often amongst the 'also rans' were the wingers Dick and Harry;
Sometimes they made a great mistake and kicked the ball away,
But most of the time they were content to watch the others play.
Clements the back was injured and Dan said 'This wont do
I must give you a dose of tonic. Guinness is good for you.'
As Admiral Fearn was tiring of treading the self same ground,
Referee Claude gave orders the teams must change around.
They had the usual interval allowed by the English League
And Harry and Dick required a rest they were suffering from fatigue.
The horsemen wanted their gee-gees to carry them o'er the ground
And the Mariners asked for a tug boat to take them homeward bound;
But trainer George and Trainer Dan of their boys are very fond
And promised them a picnic upon the Ballast Pond.
So again they crawled upon the field by Squance and Hannaford led.
A couple of them seemed half asleep and should have gone to bed.

Off went the smart landlubbers and George piped his eye
As he saw three shots in succession to the Mariners goal net fly.
Of the shots which passed by Southard one from Tamblin came
Friend was twice successful so the landsmen won the game.

The Mariners cheered the victors for seamen are sportsmen true
From the landsmen came the prompt reply 'Boys, here's the same to you'
Then they gathered at the pavilion where the landsmen received the Cup
And later it was passed around (with port they filled it up)'
The Boss gave an oration, it was plain to you and me
That he had spoken at Meetings of the Torpoint U.D.C.
He expressed the hope that George and Dan would seal another bond
To play a game on Good Friday inside the Ballast Pond.

Erect, go the curly tails of the porkers in the sty
And the gamecocks start their crowing when Dan goes passing by.
The horses in the stables began to prance and neigh
When they heard of Dasher's triumph on the field on Christmas Day.

Aboard the tugs and hoppers the Mariners often will
Shed tears as they think of Christmas and their downfall at the Mill.
But they around the hoppers will now have daily runs
And be ready to give the landlubbers some shots with Hot Cross Buns.

Go to Tamar Wharf on Good Friday and cross the beach beyond
To witness this exciting game inside the Ballast Pond.
There will be no fee for admission, but sportsmen are always kind
So give a liberal donation for the Institute for the Blind.

Finale
Of all our Yule Tide pleasures one ranks above all others
The football match of the jolly boys of the firm of Reynolds Brothers
Ferryman 29.12.35

ACKNOWLEDGEMENTS

To write the history of W. J. Reynolds would not have been possible without the considerable help of very many people. From the Reynolds family, Jill Wiltshire, Dinah Reynolds, and David Reynolds Martin; ex employees, Captains Archie Ayres and Jack Hocking, engineers Michael Morgan and Ralf Farrell, stokers Alan Wade, Russell Tinns and Alan Harris, shipwright Peter Harris. Descendants and relatives of Reynolds' employees include Gillian Ferguson (nee Hannaford), Shirley Rowe (nee Hacker), David Bradford, Murray Hyslop, Mrs Page, Mrs Barbara Medway and Lou Dearden.

Others who contributed include Captain Tim Charlesworth Harbourmaster of the Cattewater Harbour Commission, Captain Des McLinden, Chief Plymouth Pilot; Captain John Higham, retired Plymouth Pilot; Dave Warren, Ivor White, Sheila Moyle and R. Johnson.

Martin Langley, widely regarded as an expert on, and who has written many books on, West Country shipping, many years ago had prepared an unpublished manuscript on the tugs of Plymouth. It encompasses Dockyard and Admiralty tugs as well as commercial tugs owned by various operators over the years. A major part of this work was devoted to Reynolds' tugs, Martin knew many of Reynolds' men in the 1930s, and he has kindly let me utilise much of his material in this book.

Much technical information can be found in *Lloyds Registers of Shipping* and the *Mercantile Navy Lists*, but this was added too by contributions from fellow shipping historians and researchers, David Asprey, George Robinson, Piet Van Damme, David Waller, Gareth Hicks, Mike Nash and Bill Harvey.

Mike Doherty of Plymouth had the good fortune in the 1960s to be able to sail on nearly all the tugs at different times and he has willingly shared both his recollections and photographic collection. Mike has also been able to assist with much technical and local information, especially regarding the Plymouth Breakwater and block making works.

Alan Kittridge, who was originally from Plymouth, and who like Martin Langley has written many books on local passenger boats, especially in the Plymouth area, contributed much information regarding the early years and W. J. Reynolds' excursions into the passenger boat trade.

Others who were able to supply photographs have included Dinah Reynolds, Paul Richards, Dave Hocquard, Ron Stanford, Richard Cox, Captain Jack Hocking, Captain Archie Ayers, Michael Morgan, Lou Dearden, Dave Bradford, John and Marion Clarkson and the Maritime Photo Library.

Many of the photographs came from the Reynolds family, and Jill Wiltshire was able to provide not only copies of photographs, which used to adorn the company offices, but also a number included in the private family albums. Jill has also kept her great grandfather's purchase diary and other relevant papers to which she kindly allowed me full access. David Reynolds Martin has a large collection of photographs and memorabilia of the family firm, and he worked for the firm during the school holidays. David also gave freely of his reminiscences and the photographs in his possession.

I am grateful to the Plymouth *Evening Herald* who printed an appeal for information, which placed me in contact with many of the people listed above; and the help provided by the Plymouth and West Devon Records Office, making available the Plymouth Shipping Registers for the relevant period.

If I have omitted to mention anybody else who contributed please accept my sincere apologies.

When one is researching a subject such as this, inevitably facts emerge which as an author you may not have been aware of, or which give substance or otherwise to what may have been a dim recollection or story by a third party. Strange coincidences can also occur. One of my previous books charted the history of another family run tug owning firm, T. R. Brown and Sons of Bristol, in many ways similar to W. J. Reynolds. During the research on the Brown book I discovered that one of their barges had originally been a coastal steamer operating in Africa in the 1870s, and had reputedly carried the explorer Henry Morton Stanley (of 'Doctor Livingstone I presume' fame) during one of his (Stanley's) African expeditions. H. M. Stanley was, amongst other things, principally responsible for the 'colonisation' of the Belgian Congo, and the finance to support this later expedition was supplied by Leopold II, King of the Belgians. The tug *Boarhound*, of W. J. Reynolds, was built in Belgium and originally named *Leopold II* after the King!

Leopold II, King of the Belgians, after whom the Boarhound was originally named.
PIET VAN DAMME
COLLECTION

Index

Vessels

Alert 14.

Alexandra 4, 24, 26, 27, 29, 37, 39, 40, 41, 43, 46, 48, 49, 52, 56, 58, 59, 61, 66–68, 71–73, 75, 76, 81, 83, 84, 87, 89, 91, 94, 96, 101, 102, 111, 112, 126, 127.

Alsatian 107.

Amazon 49.

Andria 65.

Antony (1) 36–39, 128.

Antony (2) 42, 43, 53, 55, 56, 58, 59, 60, 61, 88, 89, 91, 92, 101, 102, 129, 132, 133.

Antony (3) 88, 92, 93, 95, 97, 107, 108, 110, 113, 114, 130.

Arion 107.

Artemisia 63.

Audrey 51.

Bahia 44, 45, 52, 58, 59, 65, 126, 129.

Bessie 12, 127.

Boarhound 21, 32, 33, 37, 39, 40, 41, 52–55, 56, 58–62, 65, 83, 128.

British Osprey 110.

Briton 21, 22, 25, 29, 34, 35, 37, 38, 48, 50, 53, 57, 59, 65, 127.

Brook 92, 131.

Cable Restorer 111.

Cadishead 128.

Camel Barge 84–86.

Cannis 110.

Carbeile 4, 8, 9, 70–78, 84, 89, 91, 93–96, 100–102, 105, 109, 110, 114, 126, 130.

Claretta 42, 59, 76, 92, 93, 131.

Clearwell 53, 92, 93, 131.

Commonweal 129.

Commonwealth 42–44, 90, 129.

Cooperator 38, 128.

Corgarth 89, 130.

Cruden Bay 38, 60, 79, 128.

Dainty 10, 13, 15, 16, 127.

Deerhound 31, 32.

Douglas 63.

Eagle 33, 34, 128.

Empire Raymond 59.

Excelsior 17.

FHC No 2 44, 92, 131.

FHC No 4 131.

F T Everard 98, 130.

Falgarth 124, 125.

Fighting Cock 62, 63, 129

Flora 42

Gallant 65, 66, 74, 87, 97, 129.

George Livesey 71, 72, 126, 130.

HMS Doris 22.

HMS Eagle 78.

HS28 34, 36, 128.

HS29 34, 36, 128.

HS30 34, 36, 128.

HS31 34, 36, 128.

HS35 34, 36, 42, 129.

Harry Herbert 17.

Hasty 41, 42, 128.

Herzogin Cecilie 46, 48, 49.

Ionic Coast 110.

Iridescence 61.

James Egan Lane 56.

Jellicoe Rose 52.

John W Mackay 97.

Jubilee 25, 26, 131.

Jumbo 16, 130.

Kathleen & May 66.

Lady of the Isles 19.

Lanesra 67.

Leopold I 31, 32, 127.

Leopold II 31–33, 128, 140.

Link 10, 13, 15, 16, 127.

Linnet 42, 128.

Lord Beresford 50, 51, 129.

Lorna 15, 16, 25, 127

Marguerite 14, 15, 127.

Mari II 55.

Mascotte 15, 25, 29, 127.

May 63.

Mona 62, 63.

Mount Manisty 36, 128.

Napier of Magdala 42, 128.

Plymgarth 124, 125.

Reagarth 92, 130.

Red Rose 21.

Reindeer 15.

Rescue 21, 22.

Rockwood 22.

Sagacity 49.

Saxon 18, 19, 21, 25–27, 29, 37, 127.

Scraesdon 32, 37, 41, 127.

Similarity 96.

Sir Bevois 55.

Sleuthound 31, 32.

Start Point 131.

Stone Bow 131.

Tactful (1) 50–52, 54, 57–59, 65, 69, 76, 77, 89, 98, 129.

Tactful (2) 4, 94, 98–102, 104, 110–112, 114, 130.

Tap 16, 22, 56, 130,

Test 93, 131.

Thames 16, 21, 130.

Tolbenny 98, 99, 130.

Torgarth 125.

Torpedo boat 108 72.

Totnes Castle 108.

Toxteth 45.

Tregarth 125.

Trethosa 58, 62, 63, 65, 74, 89, 91, 92, 129.

Trevol (1) 2, 30, 36, 37, 39, 41–43, 46, 48, 49, 52, 56, 58–61, 64–66, 71, 128.

Trevol (2) 4, 71, 92, 97, 101, 102, 105–107, 110, 114, 130.

Umberleigh 41.

Victoria 16.

Vussel 9, 43, 68, 69, 93, 104, 105, 111, 114, 115, 129.

Wolfhound 31, 32, 50.

Wolsdon 4, 16, 33–35, 37, 40, 58, 59, 67, 68, 77, 78, 94, 101, 111, 113, 116, 128.

Yank 26, 56, 131.

PEOPLE

Andrews George 21-23.

Armstrong Charlie 101.

Ayers Archie 75, 76, 78, 92, 101, 104, 108.

Bradford Dick 39.

Bradford Sam 37, 39.

Bradford Stan 55, 56, 82, 83, 101, 102, 107, 108, 133.

Burleigh Winifred Blanche 116, 120.

Butson Joe 47, 138.

Butson Les 47, 138.

Butson Reg 55, 79, 101, 108, 133.

Callow David 96, 108, 109.

Cann Frank 59.

Cann George 59.

Carter Rudge 73, 78, 101.

Clayton Captain 101.

Clements Aeron 59.

Cook Alfie 84.

Cook Bill 109.

Cox & Co 4, 19, 26, 27, 67, 89, 92, 96, 113, 130.

Crichton Thompson & Co Ltd 34, 128, 129.

Dawe Jack 59, 75, 23, 122.

Day Summers & Co 44, 129.

Daymond Stan 32, 41, 55, 56, 83.

Daymond William 32, 39, 41, 83.

Dearden Jack 67, 109.

Devereaux Dick 73, 77, 137.

Duff Samuel Hugh 16, 130.

Elford (Family) 26.

Erikson Gustav 48.

Erikson Pamela 48.

Erikson Sven 48.

Farrell Ralph 83, 84, 108.

Fox & Co 22.

Friend Walter 57.

Fullerton J. (Shipbuilders) 51, 129.

Fursland Archie 76, 101.

Gaselee & Sons Ltd 99.

Gilmore Peter 115.

Glanville Dan 59.

Grant Dicky 27.

Groggett Mr 26.

Hacker Donald 67, 75, 76, 80, 82, 83, 87, 101.

Hannaford Fred 109.

Hannaford Gillian 109.

Hannaford Steve 56, 80, 82, 101, 107–109, 133.

Hanslip C. 47.

Harris Alan 109, 111.

Harris Oscar 49.

Harris Peter 109.

Haskell John 16.

Haskell Joseph 32, 33.

Hawkins Jack 64.

Heale Jack 59.

Heard Jack 59.

Hearse Walter 14.

Herd Frank 59.

Hicks Gareth 60.

Higham John 77.

Hocking Billy 69, 76, 104, 115.

Hocking Jack 77, 94, 96, 97, 100–102, 104, 108.

Hocking Tony 104, 112.

Holland Mr 60.

Hudson Lieutenant 49.

Hyslop Murray 101.

Jenkins Mr 59.

King George V 47.

Lang Mr 59.

Langley Martin 83.

Lay Fred 76.

Leach Charlie 59.

Lean W. H. 21, 127.

Little & Co 12.

Majdalany Fred 81.

Martin Eric 52, 64, 101, 108.

Martin Terry 57.

Mead Don 108.

Medway Danny 101, 102, 108.

Metters Terry 108.

Monsarrat Nicholas 64.

Morgan Michael 70–74, 77–79, 101, 136.

Musser Christine (Rev) 126.

Palmer Ron (Curly) 73, 78, 100, 101.

Parnell S. 47.

Parson John 14.

Paul Mr 25.

Pearce Fred 59.

Pearce Harry 47, 59, 122.

Pethick Bros 22, 25.

Pole Carew (Estate) 27.

Portus Stephen 45, 44, 129.

Prescott George 82, 83, 101.

Rea R. & J. H. 89, 92, 130.

Reynolds Albert Edward 13, 119.

Reynolds Arthur Basil 11, 26, 33, 44, 50, 52, 53, 57, 59.

Reynolds Arthur Edward 13, 60, 74–79, 94, 96, 97, 108, 109, 116, 119, 120.

Reynolds Claude W. G. 11, 26, 41, 47, 54, 68, 69, 118, 120.

Reynolds Cora Ernestine 11, 119.

Reynolds Dinah 109, 120.

Reynolds George Henry 13.

Reynolds Hilda 120.

Reynolds John 11.

Reynolds Monica 120.

Reynolds Rebecca M. 11, 22, 33, 119.

Reynolds Thomas Edwin 13, 119.

Reynolds Walter Fearnley 11, 33, 26, 41, 42, 44, 50, 53, 57, 59, 74, 75, 79, 100, 118, 120.

Reynolds Walter Samuel 113, 119.

Reynolds Wilfred J. 11, 16, 19, 26, 33, 39, 42, 57, 54, 59, 61, 116, 118, 120.

Reynolds William 19.

Reynolds William John 8, 11,–17, 19, 21–23, 25, 27, 33, 39, 118, 119.

Rice Dasher 59, 137.

Roberts Charles 42.

Roberts Sydney 42, 50, 129.

Rowe William 19, 21, 127.

Seeley W 47.

Simpson Strickland & Co Ltd 10, 127.

Skinner R 47, 137.

Southard Reg 22, 67.

Spiller Tony 101, 108.

Stacey Colin 57.

Tickle Albert 57.

Tickle Holly 57.

Tinns Russell 84.

Toms Stan 67.

Toyne Carter & Co 63, 129.

Treleaven George F. 21, 31, 32, 50, 127, 128.

Tresider Mickey 70.

Tucker Henry 15, 16.

Turner Mr 22.

Wade Alan 97.

Watkins William 62, 129.

Webb Fred 57.

Westcott John 23.

White Albert 57.

White Tom 57.

Williams Buss 83.

Willoughby's (Ship Builders) 26, 31, 32, 57, 72,
      128.

Wilson Ronnie 101.

Wilson, Sons & Co 44, 129.

Wiltshire Frank 60.

Wiltshire Jill 69, 126.

Wiltshire Reg 60, 61, 66, 67, 69, 96, 97, 108,
      116, 119, 126.

Wood Dennis Hill 67.